THE WORKS 2

Brian Moses and Pie Corbett

Brian Moses left teaching in 1988 to write full-time. Since then he has written or edited over 130 books including his own poetry collections *Don't Look at Me in that Tone of Voice* and *Barking Back at Dogs* (both Macmillan). He is also a performance poet and percussionist who has read his poetry in a multitude of schools and libraries throughout the UK. He undertakes residencies at international schools in Europe, and has been resident writer at RAF schools in Cyprus and at Castle Cornet in Guernsey.

Pie Corbett was a primary teacher and headteacher. He once worked in the same school as Brian Moses where they ran writing clubs, published anthologies of children's poetry and pretended to teach maths while they were really both writing poetry. He worked in teacher training and was English Inspector in Gloucestershire. He advises the National Literacy Strategy, especially on teaching poetry, writing and grammar. He writes training materials and has run Inservice training across the country. The author of over a hundred books, a poet and storyteller, he spends much of his time irritating editors by not answering the phone because he is making poems up or daydreaming.

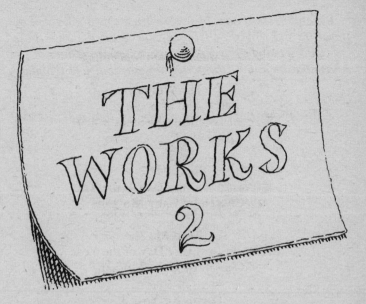

THE WORKS 2

Poems on every subject
and for every occasion

Chosen by Brian Moses
and Pie Corbett

MACMILLAN CHILDREN'S BOOKS

Pie and Brian would like to dedicate this book to all the teachers and children that they have worked with – those who set alight the creative spark, fan the flames of imagination and celebrate our unique ability to wonder.

Mol an óige agus tiocfaidh sí.

Celtic Proberb: Praise the young and they will flourish.

First published 2002 by Macmillan Children's Books
a division of Macmillan Publishers Limited
20 New Wharf Road, London N1 9RR
Basingstoke and Oxford
www.panmacmillan.com

Associated companies throughout the world

ISBN 0 330 39902 0

5 7 9 8 6 4

A CIP catalogue record for this book is available from the British Library.

Typeset by SX Composing DTP, Rayleigh, Essex
Printed and bound in Great Britain by Mackays of Chatham plc, Kent

Contents

Contents

Contents

Geography

Contents

Design, Technology and ICT

Contents

Maths

Contents

Contents

Religious Education

Contents

Assemblies

Personal, Social and Sensitive Issues

Contents

Contents

The Environment

Contents

Model Poems

Contents

The Works 2 – Introduction

This anthology is friend and travelling companion to the earlier anthology *The Works*. In that collection Paul Cookson gathered poems that related to the National Literacy Strategy. It ended up as a vast compendium of poetic forms, techniques and subjects, and has become a standard reference work to be found in most primary schools.

In this collection we have gathered poems that relate to other areas of the curriculum – notably art, music, history, geography, technology, mathematics, science, religious education and the environment. Our search was a long haul, scanning many thousands of new poems as well as those already printed. Gradually, over the months, we added more and more poems to the pile of possibilities. Some subjects were obvious favourites with writers, while others received scant attention. Of course, school is about more than just subjects, and so we also included poems that might be handy for assemblies.

While the pile of subject poems gradually became a ridge of hills and then a mountain, another cairn of poems began to grow around other themes – sensitive issues. Poems about those aspects of life that are not on the formal curriculum but have to be tackled – bullying, sharing, death, friendship, divorce, memories, name-calling, wonder . . . So we dragged these together under a section, titled 'Personal, Social and Sensitive Issues'.

The final section in the book is titled 'Model Poems'. These poems act as invitations to write. They lend themselves to children creating their own versions. They are the sort of poems that could be used in poetry workshops to kickstart the children's own writing and would be a useful annexe to the original volume of *The Works*.

So, why poetry and the rest of the curriculum? Well, the recent writing flier from the National Literacy Strategy, *Writing Poetry*, makes the point clearly. It suggests that teachers might, 'establish a positive climate for poetry through relating poetry to other curriculum areas'. Poetry has the benefit of brevity – but at its best it introduces a new slant, creates an echo in the mind and prompts questioning, wonder and thought. It can forge links between the self and that which is not yet known. It is a special way of seeing things. Other subjects such as history present the facts. Stories can help facts live as if they were realities. And poetry digs under the skin, to preserve experience, to illuminate truth. It cannot be defined – only experienced – as it is language lit up by life and life lit up by language. It has a unique voice that speaks directly to children.

This is a ragbag of poems that would be handy for teachers. We imagined ourselves back in the classroom, tugging this book off the shelf, to enrich and throw light on other subject areas. For the poet is not so much interested in explaining reality, rather in recreating it, adding new dimensions and possibilities. We imagined ourselves using that five-minute slot at the end of a session. Or using a special poem to introduce a topic. We recalled the days when making links between subjects was an everyday occurrence. And it is interesting that the Literacy Strategy is now encouraging greater integration between literacy and other subjects.

You will find the direct and simple alongside the more demanding. Do not worry if a poem seems too hard – if it is well written, then the words will cast a spell anyway. The simpler poems may also hold a charm – do not be too dismissive of the simple. Let us not be too snobbish about what children like and value. Let us present a broad variety from the immediate to the puzzling, from the direct to those poems that demand a struggle – to help the whole curriculum sing.

The poet Robert Greacen said that writing poetry is like trying to catch a black cat in a dark room. *The Works 2* is packed with black cats, mewling and miaowing for attention. Open the pages – let them purr awhile, their sharp green eyes illuminating all that they see. Let them laze around sleepily and then suddenly surprise you, slipping through the dark parts of the mind, ready to spring, to pounce, to catch that bright spark – the imagination.

Pie Corbett. March 2002.

Art and Design

First Art Lesson

My new paintbox's shining black lacquer lid
divided neatly into three oblong sections
reflects my funny face, the art room windows
white with autumn clouds and flecked with rain.

When I open it, the scented white enamel dazzles.
Inside, pure colours are displayed like blocks
of a bulb-grower's beds of flowers, toy spectrum
in china tubs and tin tubes, a cubist rainbow.

From my jam jar filled with fresh water at the sink
I pour a little liquid into each depression;
take the brush of silky camel hair; wet its plumpness
for the first time, and the last, between my lips.

Then dip its fine, dark tip into the water tanks,
and into the juicy wells of Crimson Lake, Gamboge, Sienna,
Peacock Blue, Burnt Ochre, Emerald, Olive, Terracotta,
Vermilion, Umber, Cadmium, Indigo, Intense Black.

Damp the paper. From the top edge, with sleek, loaded brush,
begin to release the first phantom of a pale-blue wash.

James Kirkup

What Shall I Draw?

Draw a house with four walls
a white fence with a gate in it
four windows, a smoking chimney –
and the path must be lined
with cockleshells and sunflowers

What shall I draw next?

An apple tree and a plum tree
a sheet of grass, pale green,
a tent made from a blanket,
washing on the washing-line.

What shall I put in the house?

A face at the window looking out,
four chairs, a table, a bowl of fruit
and in the room with the red curtains
you can draw yourself, sleeping.

You can draw yourself, sleeping.
Even when the doors are shut
you can draw your way home.

Helen Dunmore

The Paint Box

'Cobalt and umber and ultramarine,
Ivory black and emerald green—
What shall I paint to give pleasure to you?'
'Paint for me somebody utterly new.'

'I have painted you tigers in crimson and white,'
'The colours were good and you painted aright.'
'I have painted the cook and a camel in blue
And a panther in purple.' 'You painted them true.

Now mix me a colour that nobody knows,
And paint me a country where nobody goes,
And put in it people a little like you,
Watching a unicorn drinking the dew.'

E. V. Rieu

Childhood Painting Lesson

'Draw me,' the cypress said,
'I will hold quite still and bow my head.'

'Draw us,' the willows cried.
'We will lift our gentle skirts aside.'

The poppies called, 'We will give you red.'
'I will give you silver,' the river said.

I recall on this neglected lawn
How the world knelt sweetly to be drawn.

Henry Rago

My Teacher Taught Me How to See

My teacher taught me how to see
The lump within the daffodil's throat;
To look in clouds for the camel
And the bounding back of the stoat.

John Kitching

Today, in Strong Colours

Today, in strong colours,
I want you to welcome a visitor.
Give her
A purple wave
A bright-red smile
A round of green applause
A royal-blue handshake
And a yellow hello.
Place her firmly
On the palette of our friendship.

Sue Cowling

Anon.

Modern Art

It's easy – modern art is.
Anyone can do it.
Monkeys can do modern art
toads in holes
and cows with paintbrushes
              tied to their tails.
A dog could do modern art.
              Rats,
              cats,
              rabbits,
              and dead dinosaurs.
Even storks with chalks
and hens with pens
could do modern art.

It's almost as easy as writing poetry
that does not
              scan
              span
              or even rhyme properly
Or is't spelt rite.
Know what I meen?

Peter Dixon

The Museum Says

Be awed as you climb my heavy
stone steps. Built to last.
I am old by your standards.
Two hundred years have rolled past.
But young by the measure
of all of the treasure I hold.
Great books tell of kingdoms long gone
in vast rooms of old gold.
My pillars of marble reach up
to the cold, winter sky.
And my heart is of granite.
A dinosaur sleeping am I.

Roger Stevens

The Art Gallery Says

Hey. I'm cool.
My lines sweep. Zoom.
Catch the eye.
They turn beneath
a fresh spring sky.
Groovy textiles.
Razzamatazz.
This year's black.
I'm now.
Hip.
Jazz.
My wood is polished.
I have awkward seats.
Ergonomic.
White walls with crazy
coloured paintings.
Manic.
I am a bird about to rise
into the clouds.
I am organic.

Roger Stevens

I Asked the Little Boy Who Cannot See

I asked the little boy who cannot see,
'And what is colour like?'
'Why, green,' said he,
'Is like the rustle when the wind blows through
The forest; running water, that is blue;
And red is like a trumpet sound; and pink
Is like the smell of roses; and I think
That purple must be like a thunderstorm;
And yellow is like something soft and warm;
And white is a pleasant stillness when you lie
And dream.'

Anon

Jacob and the Angel

I went to an art gallery with Dad
saw a dead lobster
flame-red
lying on a telephone

some strange paintings
one of hands holding a knife and fork
eating their own insides

a man riding a rhinoceros
across the sky

then I saw these two massive men
a sculpture

one of them had wings

his hands were holding Jacob
as if he cared
that Jacob was very sad and scared

later we sat on the grass outside
had our picnic

and everywhere

that man's hands.

Joan Poulson

Matchstick King

Matchstick girls and matchstick boys
Matchstick houses, matchstick toys
Matchstick dogs and matchstick cats
Matchstick men in matchstick hats
Matchstick women in matchstick coats
Matchstick rivers, matchstick boats
Matchstick hands, matchstick heads
Matchstick dolls in matchstick beds
Matchstick houses, matchstick prams
Matchstick factories, matchstick trams

Everything is matchstick thin
But fat with life
Within
Within.

John Kitching

Who's That on the Phone?

(after Lobster Telephone *by Salvador Dali.)*

There's a lobster on the phone!

Not a crayfish
Or a seal,
Not a spider crab
Or an eel –
But a lobster!

Not a mobster
Full of threats,
Nor debt collector
seeking debts –
But a lobster!

Not a salesgirl,
Double-glazing,
Nor astrologer,
future-grazing –
But a lobster!

Not an emu
On the loose,
Nor a zebra,
Nor a moose,
Not a hangman
With a noose . . .

No, there's a lobster on the phone
And he wants to speak to you!

Pie Corbett

After Giacometti
(1901–1966)

Look –
this
man
is
very
very
thin
but
still
standing
up –
and
I
for
one
believe
that
is
some
sort of
achievement.

Fred Sedgwick

The British Museum Print Room

Van Gogh thought to be a preacher.
At twenty-one he came here and saw
the Rembrandt brown ink drawing over there,
then he did his own.

It lies in this glass case –
a splutter of rocks in the foreground,
a scruff of grass.
He drew every tree one behind the other
pulling right back to the horizon.

Dots became finer,
fields became thinner,
a track ripples to the right
while a train drags smoke to the left.

Stooks measure fields,
cypresses billow,
nothing is still.

Chrissie Gittins

Leonardo

Leonardo, painter, taking
    Morning air
        On Market Street
Saw the wild birds in their cages
    Silent in
        The dust, the heat.

Took his purse from out his pocket
    Never questioning
        The fee,
Bore the cages to the green shade
    Of a hill-top
        Cypress tree.

'What you lost,' said Leonardo,
    'I now give to you
        Again,
Free as noon and night and morning,
    As the sunshine,
        As the rain.'

And he took them from their prisons,
Held them to
The air, the sky;
Pointed them to the bright heaven.
'Fly!' said Leonardo.
'Fly!'

Charles Causley

The story is told of the Italian painter Leonardo da Vinci (1452–1519)

The Uncertainty of the Poet

I am a poet.
I am very fond of bananas.

I am bananas.
I am very fond of a poet.

I am a poet of bananas.
I am very fond.

A fond poet of 'I am, I am' –
Very bananas.

Fond of 'Am I bananas?
Am I?' – a very poet.

Bananas of a poet!
Am I fond? Am I very?

Poet bananas! I am.
I am fond of a 'very'.

I am of very fond bananas.
Am I a poet?

Wendy Cope

The Boyhood of Raleigh

Entranced, he listens to salty tales
Of derring-do and giant whales,

Uncharted seas and Spanish gold,
Tempests raging, pirates bold.

And his friend? 'God I'm bored.
As for Jolly Jack, I don't believe a word.

What a way to spend the afternoons,
The stink of fish, and those ghastly pantaloons!'

Roger McGough

The Artist's Model Daydreams

It's cold in here –
I wish he'd hurry up.

He keeps pausing to stare
First at the painting
And then at my bare shoulder –

It's embarrassing enough,
Sat here,
Cute in my birthday suit;
Not a stitch on –

And he gets so cross
If I move.
Even the slightest itch
Has to be ignored.

Bored?

Look – he's not like
That nice Mr Picasso –
A few quick dabs,
The odd line –
And it's done.
Of course,
He can't paint –
Poor chap.
His faces are a crooked mess –

And he couldn't care less
What colours he uses.

But no one loses.
The painting is slick.
Over quick –
And why should I worry
As long as he pays.

Pie Corbett

A Sort of Chinese Poem

The Chinese write poems
That don't look like poems.
They are more like paintings.

A cherry-tree, a snowstorm,
An old man in a boat –
These might be their subjects.

It all looks so easy –
But it isn't.
You have to be very simple,
Very straightforward,
To see so clearly.
Also, you have to have thousands of years of skill.

When I was a child, I once wrote a Chinese poem.
Now I'm too complicated.

Elizabeth Jennings

The Sand Artist

On the damp seashore
above dark rainbows of shells, seaweed, seacoal,
the sandman wanders, seeking for a pitch.

Ebb tide is his time. The sands are lonely,
but a few lost families
camp for the day on its Easter emptiness.

He seeks the firm dark sand of the retreating waves.
– With their sandwiches and flasks of tea, they
lay their towels on the dry slopes of dunes.

From the sea's edge he draws his pail
of bitter brine, and bears it carefully
towards the place of first creation.

There he begins his labours. Silent,
not looking up at passing shadows
of curious children, he moulds his dreams.

Not simple sandcastles, melting as they dry,
but galleons, anchors, dolphins, cornucopias of fish,
mermaids. Neptunes, dragons of the deep.

With a piece of stick, a playing card
and the blunt fingers of a working man
the artist resurrects existence from the sea.

And as the returning tide takes back its gifts,
he waits in silence by his pitman's cap
for pennies from the sky.

James Kirkup

Notes for an Autumn Painting

mist.

crisp leaves against grass.

pale sunrise.

michaelmas daisies by the railway line.

dead willowherb –
tops grey almost to indigo
– leaves burnt to sienna.

dying bracken.

saturated grasslands.

pale orange grass on hillsides, red purple
amid pale brown fallen leaves.

sky washed by the wind.

green and yellow
confetti
round silver birch trees.

mysterious rich viridian patches
across the valley.

in the foreground
grass yellowed almost to whiteness

and
a space where

the person who will no longer be in the picture
should be.

Adrian Henri

Jack Frost

He's been again
In the night
Painting windows
Sparkling white

Silver trees
And frosty paths
Crystal footprints
Spiky grass

Spiders' webs
Of wintry lace
Jack Frost's touch
In every place

Brenda Williams

Art Year Haikus

Spring morning sun bathes
Pink blossom and brave, bright birds.
I take out my paints.

Summer sun has come.
Fields of corn are gay with gold.
I paint before rain.

One bold rose remains
Despite night's slight bite of frost.
I'll save it in paint.

All is dressed in snow.
A fox pads across tight ice,
His brush caught by mine.

John Kitching

Notes

Leonardo da Vinci – a great Italian artist and thinker.

Van Gogh – a Dutch painter. His paintings were full of colour and movement. He painted people and rural scenes – sunflowers, wild skies, swirling cornfields.

Salvador Dali – Dali was an eccentric, surrealist painter from the south of Spain. He painted strange scenes that look like dreams. The *Lobster Telephone* is an old-fashioned phone that has a red lobster instead of the handset.

Alberto Giacometti – a famous Italian sculptor who created thin sculptures.

L. S. Lowry – Lowry was a painter from Manchester. You can always tell a Lowry painting because he painted people looking very thin – often described as 'looking like matchsticks'.

The Boyhood of Raleigh – this famous painting by Sir John Everett Millais shows two young boys listening to a sailor – who looks as if he is telling them stories.

Adrian Henri – Adrian Henri was one of the Liverpool poets. He was also a well-known painter and often made references to painting in his poems.

Music

Music . . .

is everywhere.
In the birds of the air.
In the hum of the honeybee.
In the song of the breeze
as it shivers the trees.
In the river that murmurs
over the stones.
In the snow wind that moans.

In the surge of the sea
lapping the shore.
In the roar of the storm
rattling the door.
In the drum of the rain
on the windowpane.
Music is here.
Filling your ear.

Ann Bonner

We Got Rhythm

Rhythm in your breathing, rhythm in your heartbeat,
Rhythm in your clapping and the tapping of your feet;
Rhythm when you swim, rhythm when you run;
Rhythm in the rising and the setting of the Sun;
Rhythm in the rain, and the chattering of teeth,
Rhythm in a caterpillar measuring a leaf;
Rhythm in a clock, and a telephone ringing;
Rhythm in a waterfall, and songbirds singing;
Rhythm in the wavelets lapping on a beach,
Rhythm in writing, rhythm in speech.

A rhythm may be noisy, or it may not make a sound,

Like the Rhythm of the Stars as they slowly dance around.

Mike Jubb

Everyday Music

All a mix together
village sounds make my music
 with horses' hooves clop-clopping
 flock of hens cackling
 wood-chopping echoing
 a donkey hehawing
 cocks all around crowing.

All a mix together
village sounds make my music
 with wind and rain rushing
 our flooded gulley babbling
 birds all around singing
 a lonely cow mooing
 rolling sea land-drumming.

All a mix together
village sounds make my music
 with fighting dogs yelping
 birds in trees twittering
 a lonely goat bleating
 hidden ground-doves cooing
 hidden mongoose shrieking.

James Berry

J is for Jazz-Man

Crash and
         CLANG!
Bash and
         BANG!
And up in the word the Jazz-Man sprang!
The One-Man-Jazz-Band playing in the street,
Drums with his Elbows, Cymbals with his Feet,
Pipes with his Mouth. Accordion with his Hand,
Playing all his Instruments to Beat the Band!
         TOOT and
                  Tingle!
         HOOT and
                  Jingle!
Oh, what a Clatter! How the tunes all mingle!
Twenty Children couldn't make as much Noise *as*
The Howling Pandemonium of the One-Man-Jazz!

Eleanor Farjeon

Embryonic Mega-Stars

We can play reggae music, funk and skiffle too,
We prefer heavy metal but the classics sometimes do.
We're keen on Tamla-Motown, folk and soul,
But most of all, what we like
Is basic rock and roll.
We can play the monochord, the heptachord and flute,
We're OK on the saxophone and think the glockenspiel is
    cute,
We really love the tuba, the balalaika and guitar
And our duets on the clavichord are bound to take us far.
We think castanets are smashing, harmonicas are fun,
And with the ocarina have only just begun.
We've mastered synthesizers, bassoons and violins
As well as hurdy-gurdies, pan pipes and mandolins.
The tom-tom and the tabor, the trumpet and the drum
        We learnt to play in between the tintinnabulum.
        We want to form a pop group
        And will when we're eleven,
        But at the moment Tracey's eight
        And I am only seven.

Brian Patten

In the Bleak Mid-winter

In the bleak mid-winter
   Frosty wind made moan,
Earth stood hard as iron,
   Water like a stone;
Snow had fallen, snow on snow,
   Snow on snow,
In the bleak mid-winter
   Long ago.

Our God, Heaven cannot hold Him
   Nor earth sustain;
Heaven and earth shall flee away
   When He comes to reign;
In the bleak mid-winter
   A stable-place sufficed
The Lord God Almighty
   Jesus Christ.

Enough for Him, whom cherubim
   Worship night and day,
A breastful of milk
   And a mangerful of hay;
Enough for Him, whom angels
   Fall down before,
The ox and ass and camel
   Which adore.

Angels and archangels
　　May have gathered there,
Cherubim and seraphim
　　Thronged the air;
But only His mother
　　In her maiden bliss
Worshipped the Beloved
　　With a kiss.

What can I give Him,
　　Poor as I am?
If I were a shepherd
　　I would bring a lamb,
If I were a Wise Man
　　I would do my part,
Yet what I can I give Him,
　　Give my heart.

Christina Rossetti

Seaside Sonata

(To be sung on the way home.)

a caravan   a travelling man   a razor shell   kiss and tell

a ferry quay   a ruffled sea   knotted wrack   a chalk stack

fish bone   wish bone   high tide   slip'n'slide

kittiwake   waterscape   shore line   strandline

a brittle star   a limpet jar   a muffled bell   a sudden swell

a falling sea   anemone

a melody   a memory

Mary Green

Drum

Played softly:
a badger's heartbeat,
mountain river,
tumbling.

Played louder:
soldiers marching,
giant's tummy,
rumbling.

Played loudest:
roll of thunder,
black volcano
grumbling.

Judith Nicholls

A Crack Band

Early morning boiler gives a bagpipe bellow,
starts to heat the water, makes it chuckle like a cello

radiators wake up with a tinging and a ping –
pizzicato plucking of a violin,

metal's making music on a xylophone,
pipes are groaning notes like an old trombone,

castanets are clacking, there's a clanging from a gong
as the house warms up and the band plays on.

Gina Douthwaite

Stereo Headphones

I'm sitting
on a train
and I'm
wearing my

Ste   reo
Head   phones

I'm putting
on my favourite
tape and pressing
'PLAY'

SSSSSSSSS   SSSSSSSSS
boom   boom
thumpity   thump
twang   kerrang
bippity   boom
kerbop   kerboom
kerrang   kerrtwang
asciddlybop   asciddlydoo
bbbbbbbb-   bbbbbbbb-
BOOOOM   *BOOOOM*

WOW!!!!
Why's everyone staring at me?!?

James Carter

45

Electric Guitars

I like electric guitars:
played mellow or moody
frantic or fast – on CDs
or tapes, at home or in
cars – live in the streets,
at gigs or in bars.
I   like
electric
guitars:
played
choppy
l i k e
reggae
or angry
l i k e
rock or
chirpy
l i k e
jazz or
strummy
l i k e
pop or
h e a v y
l i k e
metal – it
bothers
me not.

I like electric guitars:
their strings and their straps
and their wild wammy bars – their
jangling and twanging and funky
wah-wahs – their fuzz boxes,
frets and multi-effects –
pick-ups, machine
heads, mahogany necks
– their plectrums, their wires
and big amplifiers. I like electric
guitars: played loudly, politely – dully
or brightly – daily or nightly – badly
or nicely. I like electric guitars:
bass, lead and rhythm –
I basically dig 'em –

I like electric guitars

James Carter

46

Heavy Metal, Stormy Weather

Flash, crash, rock and roll,
This week's weather's been out of control,
For storming up the charts together
Have been heavy metal and stormy weather!

For drip-dropping in on Monday we had:

'Wet Playtime and the Raincoats'.
Drip-drop de bop-hop, drip-drop de bop-hop,
Drip-drop de bop-hop, drip-dee-drop!

Freeze-breezing upon us on Tuesday we had:

'Strong Gale and the Hailstones'.
Freeze-breeze de sneeze, Freeze-breeze de sneeze
Freeze-breeze de sneeze – aatchoo!

Clog-fogging around us on Wednesday we had:

'Overcast and the Mistmakers'.
Thump-bump de bump-thump, thump-bump de bump-thump,
Thump-bump de bump-thump, thump-dee-bump!

Snow-blowing down on us on Thursday we had:

'Sludge-Budge and the Wet Wellies'.
Snow-blow de blow-go, snow-blow de blow-go,
Snow-blow de blow-go, snow-dee-blow!

And boom-banging above us on Friday we had:

'Rumble-Grumble and the Thunderbolts'.
Boom-bang de bang-boom, boom-bang de bang-boom,
Boom-bang de bang-boom, boom-dee-bang!

But next week we're hoping for a new number one.
Yes, 'Blue Skies and the HOT, HOT SUN'!

Ian Souter

The Music Lesson Rap

I'm the bongo kid,
I'm the big-drum-beater,
I'm the click-your-sticks,
I'm the tap-your-feeter.
When the lesson starts,
When we clap our hands,
Then it's me who dreams
Of the boom-boom bands,
And it's me who stamps,
And it's me who yells
For the biff-bang gong,
Or the ding-dong bells,
Or the cymbals (large),
Or the cymbals (small),
Or the tubes that chime
Round the bash-crash hall,
Or the tambourine,
Or the thunder-maker –
But all you give me
Is the sssh-sssh shaker!

Clare Bevan

Song for a Banjo Dance

Shake your brown feet, honey,
Shake your brown feet, chile,
Shake your brown feet, honey,
Shake 'em swift and wil' –
  Get way back, honey,
  Do that rockin' step.
  Slide on over, darling,
    Now! Come out
    With your left.
Shake your brown feet, honey,
Shake 'em, honey chile.

Sun's going down this evening –
Might never rise no mo'.
The sun's going down this very night –
Might never rise no mo'
So dance with swift feet, honey,
  (The banjo's sobbing low)
Dance with swift feet, honey –
  Might never dance no mo'.

Shake your brown feet, Liza,
Shake 'em, Liza, chile,
Shake your brown feet, Liza,
   (The music's soft and wil')
Shake your brown feet, Liza,
   (The banjo's sobbing low)
The sun's going down this very night –
Might never rise no mo'.

Langston Hughes

If I Were the Conductor

If I were the conductor
Of an orchestra I'd choose
Piano-playing monkeys
And, as cellists, kangaroos,
A hippo on the piccolo,
A sloth on xylophone
And one giant, eight-legged octopus
Who'd play four flutes alone.

Richard Edwards

Song of the Animal World

The fish goes . . .   Hip
The bird goes . . .   Viss!
The monkey goes . . .   Gnan!

I start to the left,
I twist to the right,
I am the fish
That slips through the water,
That slides,
That twists,
That leaps!

Everything lives,
Everything dances,
Everything sings:
The fish goes . . .   Hip!
The bird goes . . .   Viss!
The monkey goes . . .   Gnan!

The bird flies away,
Flies, flies, flies,
Goes, returns, passes,
Climbs, floats, swoops.
I am the bird!

Everything lives,
Everything dances,
Everything sings:
The fish goes . . .   Hip!
The bird goes . . .   Viss!
The monkey goes . . .   Gnan!

The monkey! From branch to branch
Runs, hops, jumps,
With his wife and baby,
Mouth stuffed full, tail in air,
Here's the monkey! Here's the
Monkey!

Everything lives,
Everything dances,
Everything sings:
The fish goes . . .   Hip!
The bird goes . . .   Viss!
The monkey goes . . .   Gnan!

Traditional (Zaire/Democratic Republic of Congo)

Making Music

I'm a BIG BASS drum
booming down the street,
tapping with my fingers
to the booming bass beat.

I'm a fiddle playing music
shooting notes up high,
watching as they fall
from a music-making sky.

I'm an old double bass
grumbling in my boots,
shaking every tree top
down to its roots.

I'm a small brass horn
singing to the stars,
swimming in their moonshine
and diving down to Mars.

I'm a cymbal sitting still
making not a sound,
waiting for the moment
when I CRASH to the ground.

Andrew Collett

The Rhythm of the Tom-tom

The rhythm of the tom-tom does not beat in my blood
Nor in my skin
Nor in my skin
The rhythm of the tom-tom beats in my heart
In my heart
In my heart
The rhythm of the tom-tom does not beat in my blood
Nor in my skin
Nor in my skin
The rhythm of the tom-tom beats especially
In the way that I think
In the way that I think
I think Africa, I feel Africa, I proclaim Africa
I hate in Africa
    I love in Africa
    And I am Africa
    The rhythm of the tom-tom beats especially
    In the way that I think
    In the way that I think
    I think Africa, I feel Africa, I proclaim Africa
    And I become silent
    Within you, for you, Africa
    Within you, for you, Africa
    A fri ca
               A fri ca
                    A fri ca

António Jacinto (Angola) translated by Don Burness

The Group

There wasn't much to do today
so Malcolm and me and Ian Gray
planned how we might form a group
with me on keyboards, Malcolm on drums
and Ian who knew how to strum a C
or a G on his brother's guitar.

Then Ian's sister came waltzing in
with her friend Sharon and wanted to know
why they couldn't be in the group as well
and when we said no, they threatened to tell
some dreadful secret and Ian turned white,
said they could stay if they kept really quiet.

Then we argued a bit about the name:
'The Werewolves,' I said or 'The Sewer Rats'
or 'The Anti Everything Parents Say'
but Malc said no, it ought to be simple
and Ian said maybe 'The group with no name'
while his sister and Sharon said something silly
and Malcolm and I ignored them completely.

And I thought we ought to write some songs,
'Easy,' we said, 'it wouldn't take long
to knock off another *Hold on to your love,*
but don't let her go, oh no, no, no!
And Malc kept the beat with slaps on his knee
while I played kazoo or a paper and comb
till Sharon yawned, then got up and went home.

Then Ian's sister and Ian sat down
while we stood around and said what to write,
and it sounded all right till we tried it out
and discovered how awful it was
'Let's knock it on the head,' I said,
we'll need another year or two
before we get it right.

And later that night on the short walk home
I said to Malc that I thought we ought
to dump the others and go it alone.
We should have seen it all along,
two good looking dudes like us,
we'd be famous in no time.

But Malc said we were overlooking
one small but very important thing:
Neither of us could sing!

Brian Moses

Lewis Has a Trumpet

A trumpet
A trumpet
Lewis has a trumpet
A bright one that's yellow
A loud proud horn.
He blows it in the evening
When the moon is newly rising
He blows it when it's raining
In the cold and misty morn
It honks and it whistles
It roars like a lion
It rumbles like a lion
With a wheezy huffing hum
His parents say it's awful
Oh really simply awful
But
Lewis says he loves it
It's such a handsome trumpet
And when he's through with trumpets
He's going to buy a drum.

Karla Kuskin

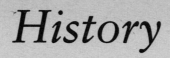

History

History

History
Is more than dusty, rusty pages
About crooked princes, queens and kings,
Or victims chained in cold and cruel prison cages.

History
Is more than the mystery
Of wars, other mighty causes
And painful pauses
For great black plagues and fires.

History
Is also your small yesterday and mine.
It is our own comic and our curious.
It is what made us small folk
Fearful, fierce or furious.

History
Is the blended thread
That binds the living to the dead.

John Kitching

Historian

(A kenning)

Time-detective
Bone-collector
Stone-saver
Rune-reader
Parchment-keeper
Villain-hounder
Hero-maker
Grave-digger
Fact-hunter
Story-searcher
Truth-seeker
Year-counter
Age-teller
Past-banker

John Kitching

The Great Lizards

The great lizards are gone,
their bones are inlaid in land, or stand
in the high halls of museums,
gaunt and picked clean, pieced together
for the cold winds to blow through.

They're quiet, these bones.
No rippling scales, no huge eyes swivelling,
no rank hot stench of heavy flesh.
Apart from these bones, we must invent them ourselves,
monsters, dragons, creatures of our imagination.

Yet the bones do not show how they lived,
but how they died; and these great skeletons,
so carefully rebuilt, do not make me think of them
striding terribly across sprawling plains
or browsing enormous mouthfuls in steamy swamps
in a world so long before us that it seems wholly alien

but of them running out of time,
fleeing across a desert where earth melts
through clouds of driven sand and ash
under a sky of smoke and fire,
closing in, burning and choking;
of them howling as their feet stick
and stumble in scorching lava
or catch in cracks as the ground quakes and splits
and they fall into the history
of two-legged soft-skinned small creatures.

And the great gape of empty mouth
asks me to imagine what
will dig us up after another million years
and raise our bones to stare at
in bewildered curiosity.

Dave Calder

Voice from the Pharaoh's Tomb

Chill winds across the desert probe
the night-dark entrance to a tomb
and metres deep within stone walls,
beyond the ears of gods or men,
a spirit voice cries out.

'How many years have I lain here?
I cannot tell, I cannot tell.
Have only known the pain of theft
from my first journey here till now,
abandoned and bereft.

Even the gods deserted me.
They, too, were thieves; they, too, took all.
They took my sun, my life, my joys,
laughter of children still to come,
dream upon dream snuffed out.

Within four coffins shut me tight,
each tomb a treasure trove of jewels:
cornelian, quartz, cool ivory,
bright blue of
lapis lazuli.

Collars of gold to shackle me,
silks of deceit to clothe my corpse,
great masks pressed close against my face,
darkness to dull the memory
of all that life had been –

the sun's warm touch upon my skin,
the Nile's soft breezes on my cheek;
my favourite hunting dog unleashed,
flurry of birds flushed from the reeds,
the boatman's echoing cry –

Chattels were all they left to me,
room upon room in crazy piles:
gold thrones and chariots, walking sticks,
sceptres and stools, rare amulets,
sad bunches of dried flowers.

And these, my cats, which long ago
wrapped sinuous bodies round my feet,
and purred and preened and licked my hand,
are brittle skeletons worn thin
within grey rotting bands.

Even these dusty memories
men have removed, men have erased.
Cold walls close in on empty space,
my soul can find no place to rest,
my spirit no release.'

Weak curses from dark shadows seep,
they wither on the desert air.
And deep within a barren tomb
a boy – a king – weeps golden tears.
Tutankhamen.

* Tutankhamen: say Toot-AN-ka-MOON

Patricia Leighton

A Liking for the Viking

I've always had a liking for the Viking;
His handsome horns; his rough and ready ways;
His rugged russet hair beneath his helmet
In those metal-rattle, battle-happy days.

I've always had a longing for a longboat;
To fly like a dragon through the sea
To peaceful evenings round a real fire,
Alive with legend; rich with poetry.

I've always had a yearning for the burning
Of brave flames irradiating valour;
For the fiery longboat carrying its Chieftain
To his final feast in glorious Valhalla.

Celia Warren

King Canute

The noble King Canute, they said
Could waves and tide abash
Canute said, 'All this flattery
Is really rather rash.
Let's make a little wager.
Do you have a little cash?'
Then he sat upon the beach, and waited. Splash! Splash!
  Splash!
Now the winds began to whistle
And the waves began to crash.
'Command it to recede,' they said
'Do try it. Have a bash!'
Canute said sternly, 'Turn! Begone!'
And twiddled his moustache
But all the time the waves kept coming. Splash! Splash!
  Splash!
'The tide is on the turn,' they said
With confident panache.
'Just give it time. One minute more!'
Canute said, 'Balderdash!
It's way above my ankles
And I think it's time to dash
'Cause I'm getting soaking wet with all this Splash! Splash!
  Splash!'

Paul Bright

Roman Invasions

BC55

Julius Caesar,
Roman geezer,
Came to Britain,
Wasn't smitten,
Back to Gaul
After all.

AD43

Emperor Claudius,
More maraudius,
Had his reasons,
Sent more legions.
They were stronger,
Stayed much longer,
Long enough
For roads and stuff,
Built some baths,
Had some laughs,
England greener
Greater, Cleaner!

Celia Warren

Julius Caesar's Last Breakfast

I'm tired this morning
Off my food
Hardly touched the olives, lark or dormouse
We stayed out late last night
With Lepidus
And talked of death
Drank too much wine
And now Calpurnia, my wife,
Is in a mood
She dreamed a death
And it was mine.

I'm tired this morning
The winds of March
Are blowing like a hurricane
Through Rome
At the Pontifical Palace
The God of Mars crashed to the floor
And what that means, I'm not quite sure.

I'm tired this morning
Upon the Ides of March
The Senate can convene without me
Yes, I think I'll stay at home.

*(On the morning of Julius Caesar's assassination, the chamber
at the Senate was full. But Caesar's chair was empty. He was
nowhere to be found. The conspirators sent Marcus Brutus to
Caesar's house to persuade him to attend.)*

Roger Stevens

Entering a Castle

Don't enter a castle quietly
   or timidly.
don't enter it anxiously,
   ready to bolt
   at the slightest sound.
Don't enter it stealthily
   taking slow and thoughtful steps,
   considering with each footfall
   the mystery of history.
Don't be meek
   or frightened to speak.
For when you enter a castle
   you should *charge* through the gate
   and signal your arrival with a SHOUT!
   You should play the invading army
   and *barge* a way through.
   You should *swagger* up to the door
   then *shove* it aside and announce,
   'Here I am! This is mine!'

This castle is here, it is waiting for you,
   and today,
     it is yours for the taking!

Brian Moses

A Sense of History

Dry were the words,
dry as the rustling page,
flatly describing extraordinary historical events;
the repeated rebellions of three princes, and
the king their father's dying rage.
The imprisoned queen was a dull figure,
silent actress on a paper stage.

But visiting the real royal castle
on a day trip from school,
metre-thick walls of cold grey stone
jarred imagination. Their senses were stimulated
by a sudden raw grasp of the reality of such rule.
Brutal spiked maces and double-edged swords
brought the youngest prince's cruel
actions frighteningly alive.
They smelled the stench of the midden,
heard squealing pigs and cackling fowl
among hovels hard by the grim defensive walls.
They saw guttering candles in draughty hidden
tower rooms, gloomy and bare, and shuddered
at the thought of being forbidden
ever to leave this damp, unhealthy place.
Ten years a captive guarded here?

Gladly they boarded the coach
for home and modern comforts,
history having momentarily come too near.

Penny Kent

The Tudors

Henry the Seventh,
A battling man,
Captured the crown
And the Tudors began.

Henry the Eighth
Was next in the line –
Married six wives,
Loved banquets and wine.

Edward the Sixth
Came after his dad –
King for six years
And a sickly young lad.

Mary the First,
A woman of pride,
Lit lots of bonfires
But very soon died.

Elizabeth R,
(Who was known as Queen Bess)
Reigned many years –
Forty-five, more or less.

With Shakespeare and Drake
She won fortune and fame,
But gave us no children
To carry her name.

So that was the end –
All the Tudors were dead . . .
Then along came the Stuarts
To rule us instead.

Clare Bevan

Guess Who?

(A kenning poem)

Horse rider
Joust glider
Music maker
Floor shaker
Tennis prancer
Heavy dancer
Diet hater
Serial dater
Dandy dresser
Wife stresser
Church leader
Poor breeder
Nifty speaker
Divorce seeker
Armour filler
Wife killer
Monk basher
Law smasher
Banquet boozer
Bad loser.

Coral Rumble

Short Livers

Some Tudor folk
Were rich and haughty.
Quite a few
Were cruel and naughty.

Most of them
Were dead by forty!

John Kitching

Cutpurse Kit

I go out hunting rabbits
large, fat, expensively dressed rabbits
with fine furs and velvet cloaks
golden clothing and leather belts.
They walk on two legs through St Paul's
or parade around the theatre.
combing their long, sleek whiskers
head in the air, eyes in the sky
my fat rabbits.

Watch me as I sidle and sneak
right up beside them
I point to the moon or the sun
through a cloud
of course they look up, twitch their noses
I take their purse
in my long, silent fingers
each knobble and bobble
a round gold coin.
Quick cut the purse strings
and it falls in my palm
like ripening fruit dropped from the tree.

I slip away
sly as a knife cut
sharp as a blade
I hear the rabbits start to squeal
mew like kittens
cry out loud for their gold
stuck in the blinding light of their panic.

David Harmer

Printer's Devil

I am the newest devil
Down at Caxton's printing shop.
I sweep the floor, I fetch the beer
And polish up the blocks.

Last week I practised inking,
A black catastrophe!
Half of it reached the letter dies –
The rest of it inked me!

Then yesterday when work was slack
Will Caxton let me set
A title page – all by myself –
And print it on the press.

The lettering was perfect,
The paper clean and white,
Except it said
   THE
   BIᗺEL
Well, I *nearly* got it right.

*Printer's Devil – a printer's apprentice, called a 'devil' because he was always covered in black ink.

Patricia Leighton

The Powder Monkey

This is the moment I dread,
my eyes sting with smoke,
my ears sing with cannon fire.
I see the terror rise inside me,
coil a rope in my belly to keep it down.
I chant inside my head to freeze my nerve.

Main mast, mizzen mast, foremast,
belfry, capstan, waist.

We must keep the fire coming.
If I dodge the sparks
my cartridge will be safe,
if I learn my lessons
I can be a seaman,
if I close my eyes to eat my biscuit
I won't see the weevils.

Main mast, mizzen mast, foremast,
shock lockers, bowsprit, gripe.

Don't stop to put out that fire,
run to the hold,
we must fire at them
or they will fire at us.

Main mast, mizzen mast, foremast,
belfry, capstan, waist.

My mother never knew me,
but she would want to know this –
I can keep a cannon going,
I do not need her kiss.

Before 1794 children aged six upwards went to sea. After 1794
the minimum age was thirteen.

Chrissie Gittins

From 'The Charge of the Light Brigade'

Half a league, half a league,
Half a league onward,
All in the valley of Death
Rode the six hundred.
'Forward, the Light Brigade!
Charge for the guns!' he said:
Into the valley of Death
Rode the six hundred.

'Forward, the Light Brigade!'
Was there a man dismay'd?
Not tho' the soldiers knew
Someone had blunder'd:
Theirs no to make reply,
Theirs not to reason why,
Theirs but to do and die:
Into the valley of Death
Rode the six hundred.

Cannon to the right of them,
Cannon to the left of them,
Cannon in front of them
Volley'd and thunder'd;
Storm'd at with shot and shell,
Boldly they rode and well,
Into the jaws of Death,
Into the mouth of Hell
Rode the six hundred.

Alfred, Lord Tennyson

Cargoes

Quinquireme of Nineveh from distant Ophir
Rowing home to haven in sunny Palestine,
With a cargo of ivory,
And apes and peacocks,
Sandalwood, cedarwood, and sweet white wine.

Stately Spanish galleon coming from the Isthmus,
Dipping through the Tropics by the palm-green shores,
With a cargo of diamonds,
Emeralds, amethysts,
Topazes, and cinnamon, and gold moidores.

Dirty British coaster with a salt-caked smoke stack
Butting through the Channel in the mad March days,
With a cargo of Tyne coal,
Road-rail, pig-lead,
Firewood, iron-ware, and cheap tin trays.

John Masefield

The Housemaid's Letter

Dear Mum,
          My life is very fine here
          Far from the village
          And the smells of home.

          I have a room in the roof
          Painted blue as a blackbird's egg,
          And a whole bed to myself,
          Which is lonely
          But so clean
          The sheets crackle like morning frost.

And I have tried
Truly
To make you proud of me, Mum.
I work hard all day,
Cleaning and polishing this great house
Till it sparkles as brightly
As a butterfly's wing.
Then I disappear down the Servants' Stair
Like a small, sweaty,
Fairy Godmother,
Unseen and unknown
By the golden ones above.

And I am happy enough, Mum.
The food is good
Though swallowed in silence.

The other girls smile
At my clumsy ways
And Cook can be kind
If the milk is sweet
And the butter cool.

But sometimes,
When the Sunday bells are ringing,
I still miss the warmth of the little ones
Curled beside me in the tumbled darkness,
And I hunger to hear
The homely peal
Of your lost laughter,
Mum.

Clare Bevan

Aunt Sue's Stories

Aunt Sue has a head full of stories.
Aunt Sue has a whole heart full of stories.
Summer nights on the front porch
Aunt Sue cuddles a brown-faced child to her bosom
And tells him stories.

Black slaves
Working in the hot sun,
And black slaves
Walking in the dewy night,
And black slaves
Singing sorrow songs on the banks of a mighty river
Mingle themselves softly
In the flow of old Aunt Sue's voice,
Mingle themselves softly
In the dark shadows that cross and recross
Aunt Sue's stories.

And the dark-faced child, listening,
Knows that Aunt Sue's stories are real stories.
He knows that Aunt Sue
Never got her stories out of any book at all,
But that they came
Right out of her own life.

And the dark-faced child is quiet
Of a summer night
Listening to Aunt Sue's stories.

Langston Hughes

My Mother Saw a Dancing Bear

My mother saw a dancing bear
By the schoolyard, a day in June.
The keeper stood with chain and bar
And whistle-pipe, and played a tune.

And bruin lifted up its head
And lifted up its dusty feet,
And all the children laughed to see
It caper in the summer heat.

They watched as for the Queen it died.
They watched it march. They watched it halt.
They heard the keeper as he cried,
'Now, roly-poly!' 'Somersault!'

And then, my mother said, there came
The keeper with a begging-cup,
The bear with burning coat of fur,
Shaming the laughter to a stop.

They paid a penny for the dance,
But what they saw was not the show;
Only, in bruin's aching eyes,
Far-distant forests, and the snow.

Charles Causley

For the Fallen

(September 1914)

With proud thanksgiving, a mother for her children,
England mourns for her dead across the sea.
Flesh of her flesh they were, spirit of her spirit,
Fallen in the cause of the free.

Solemn the drums thrill: Death august and royal
Sings sorrow up into immortal spheres.
There is music in the midst of desolation
And a glory that shines upon our tears.

They went with songs to the battle, they were young,
Straight of limb, true of eye, steady and aglow.
They were staunch to the end against odds uncounted,
They fell with their faces to the foe.

They shall grow not old, as we that are left grow old:
Age shall not weary them, nor the years condemn.
At the going down of the sun and in the morning
We will remember them.

They mingle not with their laughing comrades again;
They sit no more at familiar tables of home;
They have no lot in our labour of the day-time;
They sleep beyond England's foam.

But where our desires are and our hopes profound,
Felt as a well-spring that is hidden from sight,
To the innermost heart of their own land they are known
As the stars are known to the Night;

As the stars that shall be bright when we are dust,
Moving in marches upon the heavenly plain,
As the stars that are starry in the time of our darkness,
To the end, to the end, they remain.

Laurence Binyon

The Soldier

If I should die, think only this of me:
   That there's some corner of a foreign field
That is for ever England. There shall be
   In that rich earth a richer dust concealed;
A dust whom England bore, shaped, made aware,
   Gave, once, her flowers to love, her ways to roam,
A body of England's, breathing English air,
   Washed by the rivers, blest by suns of home.

And think, this heart, all evil shed away,
   A pulse in the eternal mind, no less
     Gives somewhere back the thoughts by
      England given;
Her sights and sounds; dreams happy as her day;
   And laughter, learnt of friends; and gentleness,
   In hearts at peace, under an English heaven.

Rupert Brooke

Growing Up in the 1930s

Liquorice plaits
And white sherbet dabs –
Gobstoppers, too –
Cost just pennies!
Picture card sets!
Coal from a cart!
Milk from a churn!
Cold custard tart!
'Bubble and Squeak' –
And black wellies!

Trousers (home made!)
And 'seventy-eights';
Thick flannel vests;
Gas-lit lights!
Skittles and hoops;
Jellies and jams;
Hopscotch and dolls;
Trolleys and trams!
'Wirelesses';
Mangles – and kites!

Trevor Harvey

Post-war

In 1943
my father
dropped bombs on the continent

I remember
my mother
talking about bananas
in 1944

when it rained,
creeping alone to the window sill,
I stared up the hill,
watching, watching,
watching without a blink
for the Mighty Bananas
to stride through the Blitz

they came in paper bags
in neighbour's hands
when they came
and took their time
over the coming

and still I don't know
where my father
flying home
took a wrong turning

Libby Houston

Remembrance Day – 11 November

Poppies? Oh, miss,
can I take round the tray?
It's only history next.
We're into '45 –
I KNOW who won the war,
no need to say.

Old man wears his flower
with pride, his numbers dying now –
but that's no news.

Why buy? –
because I'm asked
because a flower looks good
to match my mate
not to seem too mean –
(what's ten pence anyway
to those of us who grew
with oranges, December lettuce
and square fish?)
Yes, I'll wear it –
for a while.
Until it's lost
or maybe picked apart
during some boring television news
and then, some idle moment,
tossed.

Poppies? Who cares
as long as there's
some corner of a foreign field
to bring me pineapple, papaya
and my two weeks' patch of sun? —
But I'll still have one
if you really want.
It isn't quite my scene but then
at least the colour's fun.

Old man stumbles
through November mud,
still keeps his silence
at the eleventh hour.

Judith Nicholls

Notes

Great Lizards – dinosaurs are a group of extinct reptiles that lived on the earth about 230–65 million years ago. The word 'dinosaur' means 'terrible lizard' – but dinosaurs were not all meat-eating monsters. Some were quite small and others ate vegetation. They died out 65 million years ago and no one knows exactly why. It may have been due to sudden volcanic activity, a cooling of the climate or the earth being hit by a massive asteroid.

Tutankhamen – was a pharaoh of Egypt (c. 1361–1352 BC). His tomb is in the Valley of the Kings and lay undiscovered until 1922 when an archaeologist called Howard Carter found it. The Pharaoh's body was mummified and kept inside a solid gold coffin. On his face was a golden death mask. In the tomb they found jewellery, weapons and provisions for the afterlife.

Valhalla – in Scandinavian mythology, Valhalla was a great hall for dead heroes who fell in battle. There they feasted with the god Odin.

King Canute – Canute was the king of Denmark and England (994–1035). He was very powerful and managed to bring peace to England. The story is told that to silence those in his court who flattered him, he showed them that even he could not stop the tide from coming in.

Julius Caesar – poor Caesar (100–44 BC) only ruled for one year before being assassinated by Brutus and Cassius. He invaded Britain in 55–54 BC, and was killed on 15 March.

Emperor Claudius – invaded Britain in 43 BC. His fourth wife is said to have poisoned him with mushrooms so that her son could take his place!

William Caxton – was a cloth merchant (1422–1491) who built the first printing press in England in 1476 by Westminster Abbey.

The Tudors – are a royal family (or royal house) who reigned from 1485–1603. The most famous was King Henry the Eighth who is known for having six wives. Sir Francis **Drake** (1540–1596) was the first Englishman to sail round the world. William **Shakespeare** (1564–1616) was the world's most famous playwright.

The Charge of the Light Brigade – this was a famous event in the Crimean War. It happened on 25 October 1854, and Tennyson, who was the Poet Laureate, wrote this poem to commemorate what happened. At the Battle of Balaclava, due to a misunderstanding, Lord Cardigan led 673 cavalry to charge towards the Russian lines with cannons on either side of them. 113 were killed and 134 wounded before they reached the Russian line.

Galleons – these were three-masted, square-rigged ships used in between the 15th and 18th centuries both for war and to carry cargo, such as gold and silver. **Nineveh** was an ancient city.

The Blitz – was the name given to the aerial bombardment of the cities of Britain, especially London, in 1940.

Remembrance Day – this day, usually known as Remembrance Sunday, is the Sunday nearest to 11 November, when those who were killed in the wars of 1914–18 and 1939–45 are commemorated. It is common for people to wear poppies in remembrance of the soldiers who died.

Geography

Geography

I love Geography.

Other people, other places,
Different customs, different faces,
Drought and desert, field and plain,
Snow and ice and monsoon rain,
Volcanoes, glaciers,
Bubbling springs,
Clouds and rainbows,
Countless things.
Stars and planets, distant space,
Whatever's ugly, full of grace.
Seas and rivers,
Cliffs and caves,
The wondrous ways this world behaves.
So much to learn; so much to know;
And so much farther still to go.

John Kitching

Island

Firing molten rock at the sky
And shrugging water off, the island-to-be
Rises steaming from the sea
Whose waters quench its volcanic sides.

Rising mountainous from the depths,
It takes its place with continents,
Though only a speck by comparison,
Above the tides and on the maps.

A part of the world has been rebuilt,
A staging post for birds to visit
And simple plants to inhabit
Once the years weather and cool it.

The forging from the earth's hot core
Settles into its final shape:
People will find it a name;
Someone one day will put ashore.

Stanley Cook

Geography Lesson

When the jet sprang into the sky,
it was clear why the city
had developed the way it had,
seeing it scaled six inches to the mile.
There seemed an inevitability
about what on ground had looked haphazard,
unplanned and without style
when the jet sprang into the sky.

When the jet reached ten thousand feet,
it was clear why the country
had cities where rivers ran
and why the valleys were populated.
The logic of geography –
that land and water attracted man –
was clearly delineated
when the jet reached ten thousand feet.

When the jet rose six miles high,
it was clear that the earth was round
and that it had more sea than land.
But it was difficult to understand
that the men on the earth found
causes to hate each other, to build
walls across cities and to kill.
From that height, it was not clear why.

Zulfikar Ghose

Walking to School

This is the road down which I go
Early to school every day
And these are the houses on the way
Parading in a long straight row.

This is the house of the motoring man
And the car he is mending sits
Without its wheels on piles of bricks
And he's taken the engine out of his van.

This is the house with a big wide drive
With a friendly retriever
Who wags his tail to greet you
And comes to the road to watch you arrive.

This is the house you can hardly see
Among so many lofty trees
That rise in the air like fountains of leaves
And who lives there's a mystery to me.

This is the house my friend lives in:
If he sees me coming he'll wait
Hiding behind his garden gate
And try to frighten me out of my skin.

This is the wooden bungalow
Where a seagull far from the sea
Calls from his perch on top of the chimney
And scolds the people down below.

This is the house with the rocky pool,
A little windmill, a wooden bridge
And a gnome who fishes at the water's edge
And here next to it is the gate to school.

Stanley Cook

From My Window

From my window I see
the lonely tree at the bottom of our garden
waving to catch my attention.
'Come and look, come and look,'
its long fingers seem to be saying.

But I am drawn upwards,
off towards black lumps of cloud
that swagger into view
as if they are chasing trouble.
'Move over sun, your time's up,'
they appear to announce
as daylight suffers a short power loss.

Down on the streets cars are playing,
'Now you see me, now you don't'
behind the neighbouring houses
while on the distant skyline
a train rushes along chattering,
'Mustn't be late, Mustn't be late!'

Ian Souter

Houses

Where would you live if you were me?
A lonely lighthouse in the sea
With a garden of waves and rocks?
A narrowboat nosing through locks?
A windmill with a winding stair
And round rooms stacked like building blocks –
Would you live there?

Where would I live if I were you?
A wooden ark, a floating zoo.
A swaying eyrie in a tree
Would do for me.
An igloo with an icy dome,
A painted gypsy caravan,
A paper palace in Japan
Could be my home.

Sue Cowling

Building a Skyscraper

They're building a skyscraper
Near our street,
Its height will be nearly
One thousand feet.

It covers completely
A city block.
They drilled its foundation
Through solid rock.

They made its framework
Of great steel beams
With riveted joints
And welded seams.

A swarm of workmen
Strain and strive,
Like busy bees
In a honeyed hive.

Building the skyscraper
Into the air
While crowds of people
Stand and stare.

Higher and higher
The tall tower rises
Like Jacob's ladder
Into the skies.

James S. Tippett

I Live in the City

I live in the city, yes I do,
I live in the city, yes I do,
I live in the city, yes I do,
Made by human hands.

Black hands, white hands, yellow and brown
All together built this town,
Black hands, white hands, yellow and brown
All together make the wheels go round.

Black hands, brown hands, yellow and white
Built the buildings tall and bright,
Black hands, brown hands, yellow and white
Filled them all with shining light.

Black hands, white hands, brown and tan
Milled the flour and cleaned the pan,
Black hands, white hands, brown and tan –
The working woman and the working man.

I live in the city, yes I do,
I live in the city, yes I do,
I live in the city, yes I do,
Made by human hands.

Anon.

Early Last Sunday Morning

Early last Sunday morning
Dad announced we needed a glass of fresh air
and a mouthful of greenness.
So off we slipped to the nearby park
where we crept in as soundless as snails.
Around us the day breathed air
that was as sharp as vinegar
reminding us that winter was well on its way.

Inside we watched the trees stretch and wake
while the grass stood up and shivered.
Soon I was pointing towards a spider
that was strung on a necklace web
while far behind it
the sun rolled out like a golden ball.

Suddenly Dad smiled
as a squirrel scampered from a bush
then turned to grey stone
until with a flick of its tail
it waved goodbye and was gone.

Later as we passed the children's playground
I looked at the lonely, red slide
and briefly remembered the summer days
when I flew its slippery, red tongue.
But a tug of wind pushed me past
until I just let the warmth in Dad's hand
finally lead me on towards home.

Ian Souter

Stream Story

Stream in the hillside,
Burbling, trickling,
Splashing through my fingers,
Tugging and tickling.

Tumbling to the valley,
Gurgling, growing,
Pooh-stick highway,
Filling and flowing.

Bustling with water life,
Flourishing, thriving
On water, underwater,
Swimming and diving.

Now a mighty waterway,
Ships in motion,
Taking all the traffic
To the great, grey ocean.

Paul Bright

Day By Day I Float My Paper Boats

Day by day I float my paper boats one by one
   down the running stream.
In big black letters I write my name on them and
   the name of the village where I live.
I hope that someone in some strange land will find
   them and know who I am.
I load my little boats with shiuli flowers from our
   garden, and hope that these blooms of the dawn
   will be carried safely to land in the night.
I launch my paper boats and look into the sky and
   see the little clouds setting their white
   bulging sails.
I know not what playmate of mine in the sky
   sends them down the air to race with my boats!
When night comes I bury my face in my arms
   and dream that my paper boats float on and on
   under the midnight stars.
   The fairies of sleep are sailing in them, and the
      lading is their baskets full of dreams . . .

Rabindranath Tagore

The Hills

Sometimes I think the hills
That loom across the harbour
Lie there like sleeping dragons,
Crouched one above another,
With trees for tufts of fur
Growing all up and down
The ridges and humps of their backs,
And orange cliffs for claws
Dipped in the sea below.
Sometimes a wisp of smoke
Rises out of the hollows,
As if in their dragon sleep
They dreamed of strange old battles.

What if the hills should stir
Some day and stretch themselves,
Shake off the clinging trees
And all the clustered houses?

Rachel Field

Mountains

Mountains are today, yesterday, and for ever,
They have no likes or dislikes, no opinions –
But moods, yes. Their moods change like the weather.
They argue and quarrel, loud
With angry thunder. They rain
Rivers of stinging tears.
They hide their sulky heads in cloud
For days and days. Then suddenly, all smiles again,
One by one
Their magic cliffs stand clear
And brave, above a sea of white wave,
Under the lighthouse of the sun.

Ian Serraillier

The Train

The train goes running along the line
Jicketty-can, jicketty-can.
I wish it were mine, I wish it were mine.
Jicketty-can, jicketty-can.
The engine driver stands in front,
He makes it run, he makes it shunt;

Out of the town,
Out of the town,
Over the hill,
Over the down,
Under the bridge,
Across the lea,
Over the ridge
And down by the sea,
With a jicketty-can, jicketty-can,
Jicketty-jicketty-jicketty can,
Jicketty-can, jicketty-can.

Clive Sansom

Ocean Travel

If I could travel
the oceans blue,
these are the things
that I would do:

Fly with puffins
under the sea.
Dive with seagulls.
Fish for my tea.

Cling to the tail
of a rolling whale.
Leap with dolphins
in a buffeting gale.

Soar with an eagle.
Hunt with a shark.
Frolic with seals.
Fly home before dark.

Jennifer Tweedie

At the Seaside

When I was down beside the sea
A wooden spade they gave to me
    To dig the sandy shore.
My holes were empty like a cup,
In every hole the sea came up
    Till it could come no more.

Robert Louis Stevenson

Shell

When it was time
for Show and Tell,
Adam brought a big pink shell.

He told about
the ocean roar
and walking on the sandy shore.

And then he passed
the shell around.
We listened to the water sound.

And that's the first time
I could hear
the wild waves calling to my ear.

Myra Cohn Livingston

Seashells

Seashells on the beach
Are like many empty rooms.
No one lives in them,
And they're not rented out.
Where are the ones who lived here?
Whatever could have happened to them?

Anon. (Chinese child)

Points of View

More black than white, Gran's photo –
all mills and chimneys
belching smoke.
Taken from this spot, Gran says,
before her house was built.

We look across the valley
from her window –
not one mill in sight.
A colourful skyline brushed by trees.

'That's where I used to work.'
Gran points to a busy car park
far below,
then shows me on the photo:
a mill among many.
'Our work was long and hard –
deafening, too, those looms.'

Back at the window,
she picks out a bypass
skirting the sunlit town.
'Bulldozed our terrace
to build that thing.'
We examine the photo –
it's kept her blackened terrace.
'Looks dark and rather gloomy.'
'The air was full of soot –

it clogged your lungs
and specked your washing with smuts.
And as for dusting –
what a joke!'

'I'm glad I didn't live then.'
'We had our good times, too.
Went on seaside outings
during wakes* –
and people spoke more –
helped you out.
There's nothing like
good neighbouring.'

I stare across the built-up valley
and see two different worlds.
The familiar view has changed.

Wakes were annual holidays

Mina Johnson

Volcano

```
                        smoke
              heat        gas       flame
      flame                rocks           heat
              fire                                     fi
                    eee   E  eee
  i    gas       xxx X xxx  X xxx X xxx
f re            PPPPPPPPPPPPP   P   PPPPPPPPPPPPP
he            IIIIIIIIIIIIIIIIIIII   L   IIIIIIIIIIIIIIIIIIIII  gas
   a           ooooooooooo   O   ooooooooooo  rocks
l              ssssssssssssssss  S  ssssssssssssssss
   t          iiiiiiiiiiiiiiiiiiiiiiiii  I  iiiiiiiiiiiiiiiiiiiiiiiii   m
   k           ooooooo   O   ooooooo               l
s                nnnn    N   nnnn                     g
     m           E!    press   V
                RE!   pressure  VO          r
   la           IRE!   pressure  VOL
   va          FIRE!   pressure  VOLC          la
              C FIRE!  pressure  VOLCA          va
             IC FIRE!  pressure  VOLCAN
            NIC FIRE!  pressure  VOLCANI
           ANIC FIRE!  pressure  VOLCANIC
          CANIC FIRE!  pressure  VOLCANIC F
         LCANIC FIRE!  pressure  VOLCANIC FI
        OLCANIC FIRE!  pressure  VOLCANIC FIR
       VOLCANIC FIRE!  pressure  VOLCANIC FIRE!
```

Mary Green

Rain

She licked the film of dust
From her top lip.
Moved her arm across the gritty desk.
Children, listlessly worked,
Slatted shutters filtered the intense light.
Outside, the wind swirled
On the parched playing field,
A dust bowl, flanked by dry grass.
The bell rang,
Sweaty bodies ambled from the stifling room.

Exhausted,
She longed for a cool drink and shower.
As she left school,
The storm clouds clustered,
Unyielding their tantalizing promise.
Once home, Millie greeted her,
'De water lock off, Ma'am,
Must wait till six o'clock.'

A pool of clothes
Lay in the silent washing machine.
She slaked an iced Cola,
Then sank on to the bed and slept restlessly.
She awoke to strange sounds
Like falling tamarind pods,
Hitting the galvanized roof.
At first slow and intermittent,
Then with deafening staccato.

Through the shutters
She saw gigantic drops
Soaking into the dusty earth,
Watched globules of water
Form small pools on the marbled veranda.
Thunder followed lightning
And the rain ricocheted from the ground.
She and Millie ran into the torrent
Looked up and laughed,
'De rain a come, Ma'am,
De rain a come!'

Anita Marie Sackett

Coral Reef

I am a teeming city;
An underwater garden
Where fishes fly;
A lost forest
of skeleton trees;
A home for starry anemones;
A hiding place for frightened fishes;
A skulking place for prowling predators;
An alien world
Whose unseen monsters
Watch with luminous eyes;
An ancient palace topped by
Improbable towers;
A mermaid's maze;
A living barrier built on
Uncountable small deaths;
An endlessly growing sculpture;
A brittle mystery;
A vanishing trick;
A dazzling wonder
More magical than all
Your earthbound dreams;
I am a priceless treasure;
A precious heirloom,

And I am yours

To love
Or to lose
As you choose.

Clare Bevan

Geography Lesson

Our teacher told us one day he would leave
And sail across a warm blue sea
To places he had only known from maps,
And all his life had longed to be.

The house he lived in was narrow and grey
But in his mind's eye he could see
Sweet-scented jasmine clinging to the walls,
And green leaves burning on an orange tree.

He spoke of the lands he longed to visit,
Where it was never drab or cold.
I couldn't understand why he never left,
And shook off the school's stranglehold.

Then halfway through his final term
He took ill and never returned.
He never got to that place on the map
Where the green leaves of the orange trees burned.

The maps were redrawn on the classroom wall;
His name forgotten, he faded away.
But a lesson he never knew he taught
Is with me to this day.

I travel to where the green leaves burn,
To where the ocean's glass-clear and blue,
To places our teacher taught me to love –
And which he never knew.

Brian Patten

Someday Someone Will Bet that You Can't Name All Fifty States

California, Mississippi,
North and South Dakota.
New York, Jersey, Mexico, and
Hampshire, Minnesota.
Vermont, Wisconsin, Oregon,
Connecticut, and Maine.
Hawaii, Georgia, Maryland.
Virginia (West and plain).
Tennessee, Kentucky, Texas,
Illinois, Alaska.
Colorado, Utah, Florida,
Delaware, Nebraska.
The Carolinas (North and South).
Missouri. Idaho.
Plus Alabama, Washington,

And Indiana. O-
Klahoma. Also Iowa,
Arkansas, Montana,
Pennsylvania, Arizona,
And Louisiana.
Ohio, Massachusetts, and
Nevada. Michigan,
Rhode Island, and Wyoming. That
Makes forty-nine. You win
As soon as you say ——

Judith Viorst

[Answer: Kansas]

Haiku Calendar: Southern Version

In the sun's oven
New Year bakes to perfection
iced by the ocean.

February nights
with softness you can touch
like possums in gumtrees.

March dries orange leaves
on gnarled, blackened trunks after
the bushfire summer.

Like a kangaroo
this April afternoon lies
stretched in the cool dust.

From cold May mornings
the warmth of autumn soars in
canopies of blue.

Like an owl's feather
the year's first snowflake settles
into dusky June.

July holds its breath
in silent valleys muffled
by the drifted snow.

Cloud-splitting August
flashes silver rivers down
the sky's thunder mountains.

After winter rain
September like an emu
treads so warily.

October sunset:
a wedge of black cockatoos
calls wheel-oo wheel-oo.

November sunrise
feathers greying sky with pink:
galahs on the move.

Flaming December:
sulphur-crested cockatoos
dip the year in gold.

Barrie Wade

Fearless Bushmen

The bushmen of the Kalahari desert
Painted themselves on rocks
With wildebeests and giraffes
Thousands of years ago.
And still today they say
To boast is sinful
Arrogance is evil.
And although some say today that they
Are the earliest hunter-gatherers known
They never hunt for sport
They think that's rude,
They hunt for food.
They earn respect by sharing
Being true to their word
And caring.
They refuse to own land but
They can build a house in two days
And take it down in four hours.

Three generations will live together.
A girl will grow up to feed her mother
Who feeds the mother
That once fed her.
To get that food a girl will walk
Upon the hot desert sands
An average of a thousand miles a year.

Their footprints are uniquely small
For people who travel so much
To find melons or mongongo trees,
And those small dark and nimble feet
May spend two days chasing a deer.
Charity, respect and tolerance
Are watchwords for these ancient folk
Who spend their evenings singing songs
Around their campfires.

These hunter-gatherers are fearless
But peaceful,
They will never argue with a mamba snake,
When one is seen heading towards the village
They kiss the Earth
And move the village.

Benjamin Zephaniah

Design,
Technology
and ICT

Technology Lesson

We had to invent a toy
With gears and handles
And parts that swivelled
Or went up and down,
Or trundled and ran.

So I spent ages on
My best EVER design
For a shaking, quaking,
Wiggling, jiggling,
Twirling, whirling,
Astonishing, pull-along
Robot thing
With eyes that woggled
And boggled and span.

'Oh dear,' said our teacher.
'Only one idea?
Only one plan?'

So I covered a whole page
With toys that looked wonky,
Or not particularly strong,
Or useless
Or boring,
Or impossible to work,
Or just hopelessly wrong.

'Well done, dear,' said our teacher.
'That's fine.
But if I were you, I'd stick with
Your first design.'

Technology teachers really know
How to wind you up.

Clare Bevan

Excuses

Homework – to design and produce a flip-book
Materials – thin card
Fixers – glue
Specifications – 8 cms x 6 cms   20 pages
To be handed in no later than Thursday.

Dear Teacher,
Just to say,

I cut the card out carefully,
I drew the pictures too,

And I joined the little bits,
With a little bit of glue.

But my flip-book wouldn't flip,
It only flopped and flapped,

Then it fluttered to the floor,
To lie flat upon its back.

My brother in a bossy voice, said,
'Fling it over there!'

Then he took my little flip-book,
And flung it down the stair!

But it floated through the hallway,
And out the kitchen door,

And it floated up the path,
Of number twenty-four,

It found the open highway,
Without a flurry or a fuss,

When round the corner came –
A number ninety bus.

Mary Green

The Oojamaflip

Come and see! I've been building an oojamaflip.
It's easy, just follow the plan.
The widget screws into the thingummajig,
With a whatsit to hold on the fan.
The left flummadiddle clips on, just like this,
To connect with a gizmo up here.
And the whaddyacallit goes round and around
With a doofry to help you change gear.
My oojamaflip will be done in a jiff
In a mo, in a tick, never fear.
It's the biggest. The fastest. The mostest there's been.
The best oojamaflip of the year.
It's finished! It's ready! Who'll give it a try?
Don't shout all at once. Join the queue.
Just one little question. This oojamaflip.
What is it? I do wish I knew.

Paul Bright

Problem Solving

Our teacher likes us to
solve problems.
But I don't like
solving problems.
That's my problem.
I would like to invent
a way to make my teacher
disappear.
I try hard
but can not find the right solution.

Peter Dixon

Inventions I'd Like to See

A bully-pulley
A diaper-wiper
A teacher-screecher
A cold-feet-heater
A homework-shirker
An annoyer-destroyer
A sister-twister
A whiner-entwiner
A pester-ingester
A bragger-dragger
A blabber-grabber
A weekend-extender
A go-to-bed-shredder

Douglas Florian

The Song of the Engine

(Slowly)
With snort and pant the engine dragged
Its heavy train uphill,
And puffed these words the while she puffed
and laboured with a will:

(Very slowly)
'I think – I can – I think – I can,
I've got – to reach – the top,
I'm sure – I can – I will – get there,
I sim – ply must – not stop!'

(More quickly)
At last the top was reached and passed,
And then – how changed the song!
The wheels all joined in the engine's joy,
As quickly she tore along!

(Very fast)
'I knew I could do it, I knew I could win,
Oh, rickety rackety rack!
And now for a roaring rushing race
On my smooth and shining track!'

H. Worsley-Benison

Scissors

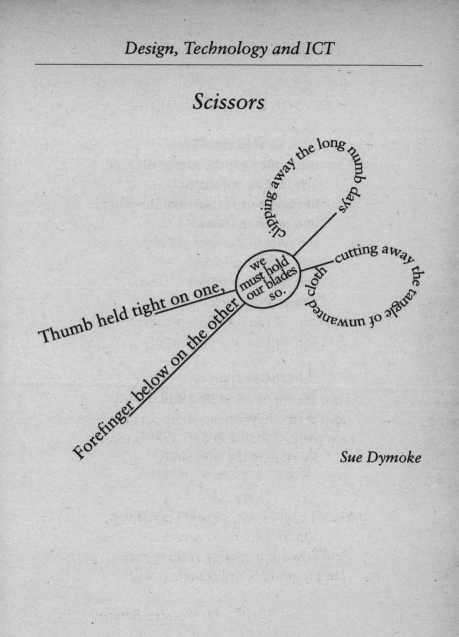

Thumb held tight on one,
Forefinger below on the other
we
must hold
our blades
so.
clipping away the long numb days
cutting away the tangle of unwanted cloth

Sue Dymoke

Go-cart

We yanked the wheels
off Tansey's old black pram
and hammered them
to make our racing-cart:
its clattering struck
the tufts of summer grass
and shook
the dusty buttercups
going up the hill.

Then letting go
we knew the hectic thrill
of astronauts
who with one mighty shove
thrust from behind them
all that they know and love.

Una Leavy

Epitaph for a Blacksmith

My sledge and hammer lie reclined,
My bellows, too, have lost their wind;
My fire's extinct, my forge decayed,
And in the dust my vice is laid.
My coal is spent, my iron's gone,
My nails are drove, my work is done;
My fire-dried corpse lies here at rest,
And, smoke-like, soars up to be bless'd.

Attributed to William Hayley

'Progress'

I am a sundial, and I make a botch
Of what is done far better by a watch.

Hilaire Belloc

Mowers

Jim's dad has a motor mower.
He says it has a mind of its own.
It charges up and down their lawn
Snorting like an angry bull,
Flinging grass cuttings everywhere.

Mrs Spencer next door has an electric mower.
She bustles up and down her lawn,
Ironing it into neat, straight lines
Until there's not a blade of grass out of place.
Her lawn is as flat as a cricket pitch.

Grandad's got a hand-mower.
It rattles and clanks as he pushes it along.
It tears at the grass, chewing it up.
Grandad's lawn looks as if it's had a haircut
With a blunt pair of scissors.

John Foster

First Television

It was 1953.
My dad had won the pools:
some pounds and shillings spare!
He'd buy our first TV.

Coronation coming up,
chance of a lifetime!
he cried excitedly.
I never thought we'd see!

And he,
abandoning his much-loved wireless,
settled down to dream in black and white
of London pomp.

On Coronation Day
I did begin to watch,
to please my dad . . .

But back in school,
to celebrate, they'd handed out
free tickets for the fair.
It wasn't long before
I grew impatient,
tired of moving images,
seen from a lolling chair.
And drawn instead by dodgems,
ghost trains, candy floss,
I walked out on those early pictures
snatched from air.

Judith Nicholls

The Electronic House

cooker. blanket.
toothbrush. fire.
iron. lightbulb.
TV. drier.
fridge. radio.
robot. drill.
crimper. speaker.
kettle. grill.
slicer. grinder.
meters. fan.
slide-projector.
deep-fry pan.
vacuum-cleaner.
fuses. shocks.
freezer. shaver.
junction box.

water heater.
Christmas lamps.
knife. recorder.
cables. amps.
door chimes. organ.
infra red.
guitar. video.
sunlamp bed.
synthesizer.
night light glow.
cultivator.
stereo.
calculator.
metronome.
toaster. teasmade!
ohm, sweet, ohm.

Wes Magee

Space Shot

Out of the furnace
The great fish rose
Its silver tail on fire
But with a slowness
Like something sorry
To be rid of earth.
The boiling mountains
Of snow white cloud
Searched for a space to go into
And the ground thundered
With a roar
That set teacups
Rattling in a kitchen
Twenty miles away.
Across the blue it arched
Milk bottle white
But shimmering in the haze.
And the watchers by the fence
Held tinted glass against their eyes
And wondered at what man could do
To make so large a thing
To fly so far and free.
While the unknown Universe waited;
For waiting
Was what it had always been good at.

Gareth Owen

New Frontiers

I am a techno traveller,
I have the gear you need
To travel all around the world
With supersonic speed.

Inside my office block you'll find
A very special room
Where all the latest gadgets are
To help me quickly zoom

Across the globe and back again,
(Though my passport is at home)
Without a plane or car or train
I'm completely free to roam,

Because I am a techno traveller,
Though I never move a metre,
With computer, fax and telephone
I'm the land speed record beater!

Coral Rumble

Mega Star Rap

I'm the king of the keyboard, star of the screen,
They call me Gamesmaster, you know what I mean,
'Cause I am just ace on the Nintendo action,
When I get in my stride, you know, I don't give a fraction,
With Super Mario I'm a real daredevil,
I'm cool, I'm wicked, on a different level!
I'll take on anyone who wants to challenge me,
No matter what the problem is, I hold the key.
I can tell you every shortcut on the Megadrive,
I can put the Sonic Hedgehog into overdrive,
And I would, I really would like to accept your dare,
But I've just run out of batteries for my Sega Game Gear.

Valerie Bloom

Spellbound

I have a spelling chequer
It came with my PC
It plainly marks four my revue
Miss takes I cannot sea.
I've run this poem threw it
I'm shore your pleased too no;
It's letter perfect in it's weigh
My chequer tolled me sew.

Norman Vandal

Hickory Digital Clock

Hickory digital dock
The mouse clicks on the clock
The clock comes on
A CD-ROM
Hickory digital dock.

Steve Turner

Techno-Child

My dad was a kung fu fighter in a video game called
   Death Cult Army
He lurked around on the seventh level waiting for smug
   contestants so he could chop them up like salami
He was good for nothing but kick jab punch gouge headbutt
   kick in the bum
And all his friends were stuperollificated when he fell in love
   and married my mum

My mum was a thirty-two colour hologram at a Medical
   Convention in Beverly Hills
She represented the Statue of Liberty and she advertised
   Anti-Indigestion Pills
She was half the size of the statue itself and the tourists
   she attracted were fewer
And if you ever reached out to touch her robes, well
   your hand just went straight through her

They met in the Robocop Theme Park on a hullabaloo
   of a night
When my dad saw off some Gremlins on Camels who
   had challenged mum to a fight
They sat together and watched the moon from
   a swing-chair on Popeye's porch
Then my father proposed in Japanese and my mother
   she dropped her torch

They were married and put on a floppy disc by
  the Bishop of IBM
Pac-Man, Count Duckula and all the Power Rangers
  came and celebrated with them
The fun was going ballistic but it nearly ended
  in tears
For those old Space Invaders started a ruck with
  the Mortal Kombateers

Since my mum's a mirage of electrons and my dad
  is strictly 2-D
You may wonder how I was born at all in this
  Virtual Reality
Well they're close as a Mouse and its Mouse-mat
  and they taught me just what I should do –
I fight video-gamesters and indigestion with
  pills and a torch and kung fu.

Adrian Mitchell

My Pet Mouse

I have a friendly little mouse,
He is my special pet.
I keep him safely on a lead.
I haven't lost him yet.

I never need to feed him,
Not even bits of cheese.
He's never chased by any cat
And he does just as I please.

He likes it when I stroke him
For he's smooth and grey and fat.
He helps me sometimes with my games,
When he runs around my mat.

I've never ever known a mouse
That could really be much cuter.
He's my extra special electric mouse
That works my home computer.

David Whitehead

Printout, Wipe Out

Our school's word processor
Can process more words
Than there are peas
In a can of processed peas.
A perfect procession
Parades across the screen.

If we're keen,
We add new words
Subtract old ones
Rearrange the order
Add a zigzag border –
Or wipe out the lot
(By accident . . .)

We've perfected
Our technique
To make ONE sentence
Last a week.

Our teacher
Thinks we're still
Learning.

We already have.

Trevor Harvey

The Machine of the Three Big Ears

*(LISA, the Laser Interferometer Space Antenna,
will be launched in 2008 and is intended to prove
the existence of 'sounds in space')*

Only part of me is metal,
only part of me is fibreglass,
for I am nothing but
a triangle of ears.

And high in the heavens,
motionless and steady,
my Three Big Ears will listen
for the waterless waves that rise and fall
across the oceans of space.

By star, by day, throughout the years
of your childhood, your adulthood,
I shall be listening for those waves
with my Three Big Ears,
my no head, my no body, my no legs,
millions of miles apart,
connected by laser beam.
My nothing but Three Big Ears connected
as you grow in body and brain.

What shall I listen for
with my Three Big Ears?

For the singing of the supernova,
for the ringing of runaway stars,
for the plug-hole suck of black holes,
for the chirrup of galaxies colliding.

And reader, in your old age,
you will think of my Three Big Ears
catching the tiny tinkling sounds of space
and catapulting them to Earth,
to the Two Small Ears
on your curious body machine.

John Rice

Maths

One Pink Sari

One pink sari for a pretty girl,
Two dancing women all in a whirl,
Three charmed cobras rising from a basket,
Four fat rubies, in the Rajah's casket,
Five water carriers straight and tall,
Six wicked vultures sitting on the wall,
Seven fierce tigers hiding in the grass,
Eight elephants rolling in a warm mud bath,
Nine green parrots in the coconut tree,
Ten twinkling stars, a-twinkling at me!

Ann Marie Linden

Two Times Table

Twice one are two,
Violets white and blue.

Twice two are four,
Sunflowers at the door.

Twice three are six,
Sweet peas on their sticks.

Twice four are eight,
Poppies at the gate.

Twice five are ten,
Pansies bloom again.

Twice six are twelve,
Pinks for those who delve.

Twice seven are fourteen,
Flowers of the runner bean.

Twice eight are sixteen,
Clinging ivy ever green.

Twice nine are eighteen,
Purple thistles to be seen.

Twice ten are twenty,
Hollyhocks in plenty.

Twice eleven are twenty-two,
Daisies wet with morning dew.

Twice twelve are twenty-four,
Roses . . . who could ask for more.

Anon.

Why Must it Be Minus Three?

When I had
Three wrong
Out of twenty,
My teacher wrote
– 3

But that's like crying
When a few weeks
Of the summer holidays are over,
Instead of rejoicing
Because there are so many left,

Or fretting
About the cupcakes
With rainbow sprinkles
That have been eaten,
Instead of admiring

The luscious ones
Still waiting on the plate.

I think my teacher
Should have written

+ 17

Kali Dakos (USA)

Numberless!

If all the numbers in the world were
rubbed out,
removed,
taken away:
I wouldn't know how old I was,
I wouldn't know the time of day,
I wouldn't know which bus to catch,
I wouldn't know the number of goals I had scored,
I wouldn't know how many scoops of ice cream I had,
I wouldn't know my phone number,
I wouldn't know the page on my reading book,
I wouldn't know how tall I was,
I wouldn't know how much I weighed,
I wouldn't know how many sides there are in a hexagon,
I wouldn't know how many days in the month,
I wouldn't be able to work my calculator.
And I wouldn't be able to play hide-and-seek!
But I would know,
as far as my mum was concerned,
I was still her NUMBER ONE!

Ian Souter

What Is a Million?

The blades of grass growing
   on your back lawn.
The people you've met
   since the day you were born.

The age of a fossil
   you found by the sea.
The years it would take you
   to reach Octran Three.

The water drops needed
   to fill the fish pool.
The words you have read
   since you started school.

Wes Magee

Time

Time's a bird, which leaves its footprints
At the corners of your eyes,
Time's a jockey, racing horses,
The sun and moon across the skies.
Time's a thief, stealing your beauty,
Leaving you with tears and sighs,
But you waste time trying to catch him,
Time's a bird and Time just flies.

Valerie Bloom

Seven Fat Fishermen

Seven fat fishermen,
Sitting side by side,
Fished from a bridge,
By the banks of the Clyde.

The first caught a tiddler,
The second caught a crab,
The third caught a winkle,
The fourth caught a dab.

The fifth caught a tadpole,
The sixth caught an eel,
But the seventh, he caught
An old cartwheel.

Anon.

The Surprising Number 37

The number 37 has a special magic to it.
If you multiply 37 × 3, you get   111.
If you multiply 37 × 6, you get   222.
If you multiply 37 × 9, you get   333.
If you multiply 37 × 12, you get   444.
If you multiply 37 × 15, you get   555.
If you multiply 37 × 18, you get   666.
If you multiply 37 × 21, you get   777.
If you multiply 37 × 24, you get   888.
If you multiply 37 × 27, you get   999.

Anon.

Counting Horrors

1 witch with 1 broomstick,
1 tooth and 1 cat,
1 cauldron, 1 spider:
how many is that?   [   ]

2 fangs and 1 dracula,
speared by 1 stake,
8 victims around him:
now what does that make?   [   ]

9 ghosts scare 12 people
in dark stormy weather,
then hide in 3 castles:
what's that altogether?   [   ]

1 monster with 10 legs,
8 toes (not a lot),
20 eyes and 9 heads:
add them up – it makes what?   [   ]

When you've found the four numbers,
write them down and then see
what you think the next number
in line ought to be.   [   ]

Charles Thomson

[Answers: 6, 12, 24, 48, 96]

A Bit of a Problem

I love my teacher
I'm going to marry her one day.
But, as I'm only half her age,
'That's quite absurd,' you'll say.

It's not as silly as you think.
Reflect upon my words:
If she can wait eleven years,
The fraction is two thirds.

If Miss can be quite patient,
Like any good man's daughters,
And wait eleven short years more,
I'm catching up: three quarters.

If life is only long enough,
Before we leave the stage
I will have married lovely Miss,
And we'll both be the same age!

How old am I?

John Kitching

[Answer: 11]

Pyramid Pie

To
make a
pyramid
take thirty-six
syllables, eight lines,
some spaces in between,
a dash of logic and mix
with a few grains of desert sand.

Mary Green

Teacher's Torture

Add two times twenty-two,
To twelve and twenty more,
Take forty-five from fifty-five,
Add four by forty-four.

Add six and six to sixteen,
To eighteen by eleven,
To nine and nine and ninety-nine,
Add nine from ninety-seven.

Add thirty-three and thirteen,
Take seven from twenty-four,
Add seventy-seven to sixty-six,
And total up your score.

You can count them on your fingers,
You can count them on your toes,
You can count them out with counters,
You can count them out in rows.

And when you've got the answer,
When you're sure, and only then –
You can add another hundred
And count them all again!

Mary Green

[Answer: 999]

Tall Story

graph

my

on

it

fit

not

could

but

giraffe,

a

measure

to

went

I went to measure a giraffe, but could not fit it on my

Mike Johnson

Mathematically Telepathically Magical

Think of a number from one to ten.
Any one will do.
Are you ready with your number then . . .
multiply it by two.

Once you have the answer
add another six.
Have you got this total?
Here's what you do next . . .

Halve the total you have got
(and this is the magical mystery)
Subtract the number you first thought of
and your answer must be . . . three!

It's mathematically telepathically magical you see.
It works with any number from one right up to ten.
Carefully follow each of the steps, your answer's always three.
Think of another number and try it again and again.

Paul Cookson

Puzzler

I am ten and you are two –
I am five times older than you.
So, my little sister, Jessy,
How come you're ten times as messy?

Philip Waddell

Behind the Staffroom Door

Ten tired teachers slumped in the staffroom at playtime,
one collapsed when the coffee ran out, then there were nine.

Nine tired teachers making lists of things they hate,
one remembered playground duty, then there were eight.

Eight tired teachers thinking of holidays in Devon,
one slipped off to pack his case, then there were seven.

Seven tired teachers, weary of children's tricks,
one hid in the stock cupboard, then there were six.

Six tired teachers, under the weather, barely alive,
one gave an enormous sneeze, then there were five.

Five tired teachers, gazing at the open door,
one made a quick getaway, then there were four.

Four tired teachers, faces lined with misery,
one locked herself in the ladies, then there were three.

Three tired teachers, wondering what to do,
one started screaming when the bell rang, then there were two.

Two tired teachers, thinking life really ought to be fun,
one was summoned to see the Head, then there was one.

One tired teacher caught napping in the afternoon sun,
fled quickly from the staffroom, then there were none.

Brian Moses

Three Frazzles in a Frimple

1 snunk in a snuncle
2 gripes in a grimp,
3 frazzles in a frimple
4 blips in a blimp.
5 nips in a nimple
6 nerps in a neep,
7 gloops in a gloople
8 flurps in a fleap.
9 snozzles in a snoozle,
10 leaps in a bunny,
some sums are ridiculous
and some sums are funny.

Brian Patten

Maths Person

'Maths gets everywhere,'
he used to say.
'Observe things.'

'Look at me for instance,
notice the spheroidal
bald bonce, the nose
fit for a hypotenuse,
the parabolas
of the bushy eyebrows.
And the clothes.
Which bit of gear's
a rectangle
with a trapezium
on each end? Clue – yellow
with blue spots. Like it? No?
Well bow ties
are worn daft this year.

Note the symmetrical
glasses, the a-
symmetrical
face. Observe
the trousers' nearly parallel
creases and behind as I rotate
through 180 degrees,
the intersecting
cool braces in red
with nattily adjacent
and also opposite
angles. *Spot*
the elliptical
hole in the right sock.'

Lesson over. Spheroidal
head gleaming, he walks a straight
shortest-distance-between-two-points
down the corridor, the elliptical
hole in the right sock
winking at us.
We notice this year
shoe-heels are worn
nearly triangular.

Robert Hull

The Unit of Sleep

I measure fun in grandads –
The best slide in the park is three whole grandads long.

I measure ponds in duckfuls –
This is a lake. Tons of ducks. Swans. Green mud, good pong.

Picnics are weighed in chocolate biscuits –
Don't care if they do melt, so long as there's a lot.

Holidays stretch in miles of sunshine –
Sand, seaslap, shingle. Donkey smell and leather. Hot.

Journeys are times in songs and stories –
From here to Aunt Em's house the wicked witch schemes
And as we arrive there, the Princess rescues Snow White.

The unit of sleep is dreams.

Jan Dean

If I Were a Shape

If I were a shape
I'd be a rectangle,
I'd be a snooker table with Steve Davies potting the black,
I'd be a football pitch where Spurs would always be winning,
I'd be a chocolate bar that you could never finish,
If I were a rectangle.

If I were a circle,
I'd be a hoop rolling down a mountainside,
I'd be a wheel on a fast Ferrari,
I'd be a porthole in Captain Nemo's submarine,
If I were a circle.

If I were a cone,
I'd be a black hat on a wicked witch's head,
I'd be a warning to motorists, one of thousands,
I'd be a tooth in a T Rex's jaw,
If I were a cone.

But if I were a star . . .
I'd be Robbie Williams!

Brian Moses

Counting

To count myself
Is quickly done.
There's never more of me
Than one.

Counting bears
Is fun by ones
But funnier in pairs.

Counting the birds
On the branches of trees
Is hard on the neck
But it's easy on the knees.

It's even harder
Counting leaves
Than counting tiny birds.
They shift their shadows
With the breeze
Among the branches
Of the trees
More numerous
Than whispered words.

Counting fingers
And counting toes is
A harder kind of counting
Than counting noses.

Counting rabbits running
Rabbit races on the lawn
Must be done while one is sunning
And before a rabbit's gone.

Counting the stars
As they glitter bright white
Is lovely indeed
And a marvellous sight
When the air is as fresh
As the first night in fall.
But I always have a feeling
That comes very softly stealing
When my head with stars is reeling
That I didn't count them all.

Karla Kuskin

Science

Up in Smoke

Cornelius loved Chemistry
It had a strange attraction
The final words he spoke were 'Sir?
Is this a chain reaction?'

Paul Bright

Earth's Clock

Imagine that the earth was shaped
Twenty-four hours ago,
Then at 6 a.m. rains fell from the skies
To form the seas below.
At 8 a.m. in these soupy seas
The first signs of life appeared.
The dinosaurs called seventy minutes ago
But at twenty to twelve disappeared.
Man arrived just one minute ago
Then at thirty seconds to midnight,
Raised himself from his stooping stance
And started walking upright.
In the thirty seconds man's walked the earth
See what he's managed to do.

Earth's clock continues ticking;
The rest is up to you.

Pat Moon

Freddie Fox, Sally Sisson and Raymond Rix

Here lies the body
Of Sally Sisson.
Big explosion:
Didn't listen.

Here lies the body
Of Raymond Rix:
Was sure those chemicals
Would mix.

Here lies the body
Of Freddie Fox.
Water plus cable?
Nasty shocks!

John Kitching

Summer Storm

Light travels, said Miss,
Faster than sound.
Next time there's a storm,
When you see the lightning,
Start counting slowly in seconds.
If you divide
The number of seconds by three,
It will tell you
How many kilometres you are
From the centre of the storm.

Two nights later
I was woken
By the lashing rain,
The lightning
And the thunder's crash.

I lay,
Huddled beneath the sheet,
As the rain poured down
And lightning lit up the bedroom,
Slowly counting the seconds,
Listening for the thunder
And calculating the distance
As the storm closed in –

Until,
With a blinding flash
And a simultaneous ear-splitting crash,
The storm passed
Directly overhead.

And I shook with fright
As the storm passed on,
Leaving the branches shuddering
And the leaves weeping.

John Foster

Constant, Constant Little Light

Constant, constant, little light,
catch my eye in darkest night.
What can speed so fast, so high,
laser like across the sky?

When the sleepy sun has set
and the night has cast her net.
It's then your orbit forms a ring,
round the earth a song to sing.

Constant, constant little light,
I know you're a satellite.

Cruising, spinning, seldom seen,
beaming pictures to our screens.
Weather-watching, tracking storms,
plotting maps and all life forms.

Scanning, spying from above,
are you hawk or are you dove?
Silent, stealthy space age Thor,
armed with weapons for a real star war.

From your tiny, silver glow,
who can tell what wrongs may flow.
But for now I hold you bright,
constant, constant little light.

Constant, constant, little light,
I know you're a satellite.

John Rice

Information for Travellers

As you read this poem you are on a spacecraft
travelling at sixty-six thousand miles an hour.
It spins as it flies: since you began to read
it has already turned nine miles to the east.
Be honest, you didn't feel a thing.
You are orbiting a star, not a very big one
compared to many of the ten thousand million others
that go round on the same galactic wheel,
and are flying at a height above its surface
of some ninety-three million miles.
We hope to cruise at this distance for another
eight thousand million years. What happens then
is anybody's guess. Despite its speed and size
this craft is a space station, a satellite, not designed
for interstellar flight. Its passengers
rely on the comfort of a pressurized cabin

to enjoy the voyage. We must advise you that,
in the event of collision, loss of atmosphere,
or any alteration in course which may result
in overheating or extreme cold, this craft is not
equipped with parachutes or emergency exits.
On a brighter note, the spaceship contains
an enormous variety of in-flight magazines,
meals to suit every taste, and enough
games, puzzles and adventures
to last a lifetime.
We hope you enjoy your voyage.
Thank you for flying Planet Earth.

Dave Calder

Chalk

As we walk across this hill of chalk
It's hard to imagine
That once these hills
Were below the sea
That chalk is the sediment
Left by a million tiny creatures
On the sea bed
It's hard to imagine
As we walk upon this thin skin
Of earth and grass
Beneath a blue sky
And a burning sun.

Roger Stevens

Science Lesson

We've done 'Water' and 'Metals' and 'Plastic',
today it's the turn of 'Elastic':
Sir sets up a test . . .
Wow, that was the best –
he whizzed through the window. Fantastic!

Mike Johnson

experiment

at school we're doing growing things
  with cress.
sprinkly seeds in plastic pots
  of cotton wool.

Kate's cress sits up on the sill
  she gives it water.
mine is shut inside the cupboard
  dark and dry.

now her pot has great big clumps
  of green
mine hasn't.
Mrs Martin calls it Science
  I call it mean.

Danielle Sensier

Star Turn

Ladies *and* Gentlemen
We are proud to present
On this auspicious occasion
The one, the only,
The amazing,
The tremendous,
The sensational,
The eighth wonder of the world,
In all its phenomenal glory . . .
MY BODY
(Plus, of course, its clothes).

Marvel with me, if you will,
At the chambers of my heart
(With their cunning one-way doors)
Pumping my blood around
100,000 times
Every single day.

And don't you have to admire
My more than 200 bones,
600 muscles,
25,000, yes *25,000*,
Cells in my brilliant brain.

And for our grand finale
I request
Silence.
Lower the house lights, please
For a live demonstration
Of something *beyond belief*.
Prepare yourselves for the sight,
Wondrous to behold,
Of this stretchy waterproof bag
That I've come to know as
My Skin.

Isn't it fantastic how something so thin
Can hold so much in?

Frances Nagle

Breath

I breathe in –
And an ocean flows through my body.
I breathe out –
And it drains away, unseen;
Leaving me
To wait
Until the next breath
Floods me with life again.

Trevor Harvey

The Shark

A treacherous monster is the Shark,
He never makes the least remark.

And when he sees you on the sand,
He doesn't seem to want to land.

He watches you take off your clothes,
And not the least excitement shows.

His eyes do not grow bright or roll,
He has astounding self-control.

He waits till you are quite undressed,
And seems to take no interest.

And when towards the sea you leap,
He looks as if he were asleep.

But when you once get in his range,
His whole demeanour seems to change.

He throws his body right about
And his true character comes out.

It's no use crying or appealing,
He seems to lose all decent feeling.

After his warning you will wish
To keep clear of this treacherous fish.

His back is black, his stomach white,
He has a very dangerous bite.

Lord Alfred Douglas

Gannet Diving

Beak,
harpoon, or cocktail stick.

Neck,
brushed yellowy snowbridge.

Wings,
a flash of glassy light,
tipped black as school socks.

Tail,
a trailing shirt tail,
freshly ironed.

Dives,
a white arrowhead
speeding from silk blue sky
to ice blue water.

Rises,
from white frothy broth
with wriggling silver prize.

Gulps,
goes for gold.

John Rice

Luck

Bedraggled feathers are uneasy
on the eye. Yet here was this little hen
being washed in a bowl, the woman
cupping her hands, spilling
the water over the bird, gently
as with a newborn child. There was no struggle.
The towel wrap, the soft blow-dry
were beauty salon pleasures. And the finished,
fluffed-up, white creation
stayed content in the holding hands. She was
keeping close to love. close to luck.

Madeline Munro

Wonder Birds

In the forest's shadows
jewelled hummingbirds
wordsearch vibrant flowers;
up, down, across, diagonally,
backwards and forwards they fly.

Their tiny, rotor blade wings
make music on air.
They hover and sip,
hover and sip,
knitting patterns of words
across sheets of leaves:

```
                    s
                    w
                    i
                    f
        d e l i c a t e
        e
        f a n s
        t
          h
            g           m
              i       e
                    r
              c       b
                    u
        m       r
          i   r
        l       a
                  c
                    l
                      e
                        s
```

Patricia Leighton

Snail

Steady explorer
you crawl on your stomach foot
   along silver trails;
stretch your soft neck, grasp a leaf
rasp it with sandpaper tongue.

Patricia Leighton

Mouse Laughing

Have you ever heard Mouse laugh?
You'd be surprised.
It doesn't sound as you'd suppose.
No it doesn't.
No squeaks, no twitterings,
No pussy-footing around.
More of a belly laugh, really.
Like the trumpeting howl of an elephant
Thudding across the parched plains of Africa,
Or the deep-throated rumble of the earth
At its centre.
You needn't believe me, of course.
But, next time you meet Mouse,
Don't tickle him.

Mary Greeen

The Day's Eye

The sun rises,
surprises the weary night,
like a sudden joke.
Daylight.

The sun gleams,
beams kindly heat
like an oven's plate.
Streets sweat.

The sun sneaks,
peeks through misty cloud,
like a sly thief,
alone in a crowd.

The sun sleeps,
creeps into cool shade,
like a honey cat.
Shadows fade.

The sun slips,
dips into night,
like a closing mouth,
swallowing light.

Pie Corbett

Winter Seeds

All among the leaf litter
lie the winter seeds,
acorns, beech nuts, conkers, berries;
seeds from garden weeds.

All the long, cold winter
through frost, hail, sleet and snow,
seeds wait, nestling near the earth,
for the time when they can grow.

Penny Kent

Mushrooms

The night before a great moon full of honey
Had flowed up behind the hills and poured across the fields.

The leaves were rusting, the wheat whispered
Dry and gold in the wind's hands.

Andrew and I went to Foss. We drove over the hills
That were blustery with huge gusts of sunlight.

We stopped and walked to the loch, left two trails
Through the grass, came on the mushrooms by accident,

A village of strewn white hats,
The folds of their gills underneath as soft as skin.

We almost did not want to take them, as if
It would be theft – wronging the hills, the trees, the grass.

But in the end we did, we picked them with reverence;
And they broke like bread between our hands, we carried
whole armfuls home,

Pieces of field, smelling of earth and autumn;
A thanksgiving, a blessing.

Kenneth C. Steven

The Hedgehog

Far too cold
For things to grow –
Too much frost
And too much snow;
Too much wind
And too much rain –
Time I went
To sleep again!
Curled up small
(Quite snug and warm),
I'll be safe
From wind and storm.

See you next spring!

Trevor Harvey

Dandelions

Dandelions shout
Barmaid fashion,
'We're out!'
And suddenly winter's gone.
They display together
Sunshine bright,
In bitter weather,
Flaunting their generous gold
Until they're old.
Ghosts in summer
They set their silken seeds
And grow with joy
To be another gallant flowering hoi polloi.
Even the leaves are edible.
Dandelions are incredible.

Gwen Dunn

The Wobbling Rainbow

Why don't rainbows
  wobble in the wind?
How can tuna
  end up tinned?
Why do airwaves
  not make a sound?
How can a mole
  make a hole
    underground?
Why don't we drop
  off the face
    of the earth?
Why does difference
  cause such mirth?
Why do magnets
  stick together?
Why do snails like
  rainy weather?
Why would an eel
  give a nasty shock?
Why does water
  turn hard as rock?
Why does my mind
  keep wondering why?
Where do we begin,
  and what happens when we die?

Pie Corbett

Religious
Education

I Thank You Lord

I thank you Lord, for knowing me
    better than I know myself,
And for letting me know myself
    better than others know me.
Make me, I ask you then,
    better than others know me.
Make me, I ask you then,
    better than they suppose,
And forgive me for what they do not know.

A Muslim prayer

Before the Paling of the Stars

Before the paling of the stars,
   Before the winter morn,
   Before the earliest cock-crow,
Jesus Christ was born:
   Born in a stable,
   Cradles in a manger,
In the world His hands had made
   Born a stranger.

Priest and King lay fast asleep
   In Jerusalem;
Young and old lay fast asleep
   In crowded Bethlehem;
Saint and Angel, ox and ass,
   Kept a watch together,
   Before the Christmas daybreak
   In the winter weather.

Jesus on His Mother's breast
   In the stable cold,
Spotless Lamb of God was He,
   Shepherd of the fold:
Let us kneel with Mary Maid,
   With Joseph bent and hoary,
With Saint and Angel, ox and ass,
   To hail the King of Glory.

Christina Rossetti

Innocent's Song

Who's that knocking on the window,
Who's that standing at the door,
What are all those presents
Lying on the kitchen floor?

Who is the smiling stranger
With hair as white as gin,
What is he doing with the children
And who could have let him in?

Why has he rubies on his fingers,
A cold, cold crown on his head,
Why, when he caws his carol,
Does the salty snow run red?

Why does he ferry my fireside
As a spider on a thread,
His fingers made of fuses
And his tongue of gingerbread?

Why does the world before him
Melt in a million suns,
Why do his yellow, yearning eyes
Burn like saffron buns?

Watch where he comes walking
Out of the Christmas flame,
Dancing, double-talking:

Herod is his name.

Charles Causley

Dedicating a Baby
(from the pygmy tradition)

Life is a tree – rooted in the earth,
An old tree – our family tree.

God planted the tree –
He makes it grow
Strong roots,
Wide branches.

And now we bring this baby,
A bud on the great tree

All life is God's life
And the life in this baby is God's life.

We – the roots and branches of the ancient tree
Offer this new bud baby to our Creator God.

Together we will grow.

Jan Dean

Disembarkation Chorus

So disembark! The storm has found its ending,
The rains have poured their very selves away,
The rocks are all a-gleaming and a-blending,
And we shall step ashore this very day

On Ararat,
On Ararat,
Sweet Ararat, the golden.

Ashore! Ashore! All birds! All flies! All fishes!
And every kind of animal, give way
To Captain Noah, and obey his wishes,
For he has found safe anchorage today

On Ararat,
On Ararat,
Sweet Ararat, the golden.

Praise be to all the Angels and the Voices,
Praise be to this great sun that burns the rain,
Praise be to Rainbows when the heart rejoices
To see the colours of the world again

On Ararat,
On Ararat,
Sweet Ararat, the golden.

Mervyn Peake

Psalm 150

O praise God in his holiness: praise him
   in the firmament of his power.
Praise him in his noble acts: praise him
   according to his excellent greatness.
Praise him in the sound of the trumpet:
   praise him upon the lute and harp.
Praise him in the cymbals and dances:
   praise him upon the strings and pipe.
Praise him upon the well-tuned cymbals:
   praise him upon the loud cymbals.
Let every thing that hath breath:
   praise the Lord

King James Bible

Psalm 23
A Psalm of David

The Lord *is* my shepherd; I shall not want.

He maketh me to lie down in green pastures: he leadeth me beside the still waters.

He restoreth my soul: he leadeth me in the paths of righteousness for his name's sake.

Yea, though I walk through the valley of the shadow of death, I will fear no evil: for thou *art* with me; thy rod and thy staff they comfort me.

Thou preparest a table before me in the presence of mine enemies: thou anointest my head with oil; my cup runneth over.

Surely goodness and mercy shall follow me all the days of my life: and I will dwell in the house of the LORD for ever.

Psalm 23:1–6
King James Bible

From 'The Sermon on the Mount'

Blessed are the poor in spirit:
For theirs is the kingdom of heaven.

Blessed are they that mourn:
For they shall be comforted.

Blessed are the meek:
For they shall inherit the earth.

Blessed are they which do hunger and thirst after righteousness:
For they shall be filled.

Blessed are the merciful:
For they shall obtain mercy.

Blessed are the pure in heart:
For they shall see God.

Blessed are the peacemakers:
For they shall be called the children of God.

Blessed are they which are persecuted for righteousness' sake:
For theirs is the kingdom of heaven.

King James Bible

In the Beginning

God said WORLD
and the world spun round,
God said LIGHT
and the light beamed down,
God said LAND
and the sea rolled back,
God said NIGHT
and the sky went black.

God said LEAF
and the shoot pushed through,
God said FIN
and the first fish grew,
God said BEAK
and the big bird soared,
God said FUR
and the jungle roared.

God said SKIN
and the man breathed air,
God said BONE
and the girl stood there,
God said GOOD
and the world was great,
God said REST
and they all slept late.

Steve Turner

Prayer for When I'm Cross

Dear Jesus, when I feel my black bad temper
Bristle in me like a porcupine
Lay your gentle hand upon my anger
And soften every spiteful prickly spine.

Jan Dean

Dipa (The Lamp)

(A song for Divali)

Light the lamp now.
Make bright
the falling night
wrapped in the leaves
of autumn.

Gone is the day.
Kindle the flame
to burn
in the dark.
Let it show
the way.

Lit is the lamp
of the moon.
Brilliant the stars.
Make them shine.
Let them unite.
Let there be light.

Ann Bonner

Plague Frog

I am
   the frog
      that leapt
         from the Nile
            that hopped
               to the palace
                  that flipped
                     to the bedroom
                        that slipped
                           in the sheet
                          that flopped
                             with a smile
                               then nipped
                                 at the feet
                                  of the king who
                                     kept Moses in Egypt.

Judith Nicholls

Jonah and the Whale

Well, to start with
It was dark
So dark
You couldn't see
Your hand in front of your face;
And huge
Huge as an acre of farmland.
How do I know?
Well, I paced it out
Length and breadth
That's how.
And if you was to shout
You'd hear your own voice resound,
Bouncing along the ridges of its stomach,
Like when you call out
Under a bridge
Or in an empty hall.
Hear anything?
No not much,
Only the normal

Kind of sounds
You'd expect to hear
Inside a whale's stomach;
The sea swishing far away,
Food gurgling, the wind
And suchlike sounds;
Then there was me screaming for help,
But who'd be likely to hear,
Us being miles from
Any shipping lines
And anyway
Supposing someone did hear,
Who'd think of looking inside a whale?
That's not the sort of thing
That people do.
Smell? I'll say there was a smell.
And cold. The wind blew in
Something terrible from the South
Each time he opened his mouth
Or took a swallow of some tit bit.
The only way I found
To keep alive at all
Was to wrap my arms
Tight around myself
And race from wall to wall.
Damp? You can say that again;
When the ocean came sluicing in
I had to climb his ribs
To save myself from drowning.
Fibs? You think I'm telling you fibs,

I haven't told the half of it brother.
I'm only giving a modest account
Of what these two eyes have seen
And that's the truth on it.
Here, one thing I'll say
Before I'm done –
Catch me eating fish
From now on.

Gareth Owen

Hindu Poem

Sky so bright
Blue and light
Stars – how many have you?
Countless stars
Countless times
Shall our God be praised now.
Forest green
Cool, serene,
Leaves – how many have you?
Countless leaves
Countless times
Shall our God be praised now.

Anon.

Hunting the Leaven

Passover

Take a candle, take a feather,
hunt in every crack.
Find each piece of leavened food
and quickly bring it back.

We'll clean our home from top to bottom,
clear out all the yeast.
And then we'll lay the table
for our special Seder feast.

Tony Mitton

Ramadan

The moon that once was full, ripe and golden,
Wasted away, thin as the rind of a melon,
Like those poor whom sudden ill fortune
Has wasted away like a waning moon.

Like the generous who leave behind
All that was selfish and unkind,
The moon comes out of the tent of the night
And finds its way with a lamp of light.

The lamp of the moon is relit
And the hungry and thirsty
In the desert or the city
Make a feast to welcome it.

Stanley Cook

Mela

Listen to the reading,
   listen to the hymn.
Today it is a holy day.
   Let us think of him
who guided us
   and brought us
from darkness
   into light –
into sudden morning
   out of thick night.

Let us eat together.
   Let us take our ease.
Let us throw our weapons down.

Here, is peace.

Jean Kenward

Light the Festive Candles

(For Hanukkah)

Light the first of eight tonight –
the farthest candle to the right.

Light the first and second, too,
when tomorrow's day is through.

Then light three, and then light four –
every dusk one candle more

Till all eight burn bright and high,
honouring a day gone by

When the Temple was restored,
rescued from the Syrian lord,

And an eight-day feast proclaimed –
The Festival of Lights – well named

To celebrate the joyous day
when we regained the right to pray
to our one God in our own way.

Aileen Fisher

Assemblies

It's a Wonderful World, but They Made a Few Mistakes

It's a wonderful world, but they made a few mistakes.
Like leaving out unicorns and putting in snakes.
Like no magic carpets, no wishing wells, no genies.
Like good guys getting picked on by the meanies.
Like arithmetic, especially multiplication.
Like expecting a person to stay at home for one whole week
   with a sitter while that person's mother and father take a
   vacation.
Like needing to finish the green beans to get the dessert.
Like everyone caring *way too much* about dirt.
Like letting there by a cavity in a tooth.
Like calling it a lie when all that this person has done is not
   mention part of the truth.
Like raining on soccer games, and liver for supper.
Like bunk beds where the younger person always gets stuck
   with the lower and the older person always gets the upper.
Like leaving out mermaids and putting in splinters and bee
   stings and wars and tornadoes and stomach aches.

It's a wonderful world, but they made a few mistakes.

Judith Viorst

The World with its Countries

The world with its countries,
Mountains and seas,
People and creatures,
Flowers and trees,
The fish in the waters,
The birds in the air
Are calling to ask us
All to take care.

These are our treasures,
A gift from above,
We should say thank you
With a care that shows love
For the blue of the ocean,
The clearness of air,
The wonder of forests
And the valleys so fair.

The song of the skylark,
The warmth of the sun,
The rushing of clear streams
And new life begun
Are gifts we should cherish,
So join in the call
To strive to preserve them
For the future of all.

John Cotton

Thanksgiving

Thank You
   for all my hands can hold –
     apples red,
      and melons gold,
       yellow corn
        both ripe and sweet,
        peas and beans
         so good to eat!

Thank You
   for all my eyes can see –
     lovely sunlight,
      field and tree,
       white cloud-boats
       in sea-deep sky,
        soaring bird
         and butterfly.

Thank You
   for all my ears can hear –
     birds' song echoing
      far and near,
       songs of little
        stream, big sea,
         cricket, bullfrog,
         duck and bee!

Ivy O. Eastwick

All in the Mind

Peace is a bird,
white-feathered
as a winter tree
frothed in snow.

It is silence
leaking from cupped
hands like ice-cold
mountain water.

Peace is a petal
on the summer wind,
fine-spun as a
dragonfly's wing.

It is a promise
straddling the skies
like a rainbow
after the storm.

Moira Andrew

Job Description

A very special person
For a very special post.
Someone who knows how to cook,
(Especially beans on toast.)
Someone who can clean the house
And drive children to school,
And buy the food and clothes and shoes
And use most household tools.
A teacher of all subjects,
A referee of fights,
Who, as relief from boredom,
Is an 'on call' nurse at night.
A hairdresser and swimming coach,
At ease with dogs and cats,
(And hamsters, rabbits, fish and snakes,
Stick insects, birds and rats!)
Has laundry skills, a taxi cab,
Makes costumes for school plays.
Who *never* goes off duty
And whom no one *ever* pays.

Daphne Kitching

Books for All Reasons

the reason i like chocolate
is i can lick my fingers
and nobody tells me i'm not polite

i especially like scarey movies
cause i can snuggle with mommy
or my big sister and they don't laugh

i like to cry sometimes cause
everybody says 'what's the matter
don't cry'

and i like books
for all those reasons
but mostly cause they just make me happy

and i really like
to be happy

Nikki Giovanni

The Dawdling Dog

From the West African Myth of Creation

Said Chuku, Creator of the world
And everything in it,
My children will live forever
And thrive
But when they appear to die
They must lie on the ground
To be covered in ashes
And then they will revive.

Said Chuku to his new creation – Dog
Tell my children what to do
So that they will never die.
Go do as I bid.

But, dear child, the Dog dawdled
Dog dawdled
He did.

Said Chuku to his new creation – Sheep
Tell my children what to do
So that they will never die.
Go do as I ask.
But, quite frankly, Sheep wasn't up to the task
And, his thinking being rather woolly,
He said to the children of Chuku –
When you die, dig a hole
A hole for the dead.
And when the children asked why
Sheep said, It's good for the soul.

When Dog arrived late
And said to Chuku's children, No!
You must lay the dead on the ground
And cover them in ashes
And they will revive –
The children laughed and said,
Who are you trying to kid?
Sheep told us the truth.

And that is why
The children of Chuku
Grow old and die.
For Dog dawdled,
He dawdled
He did.

Roger Stevens

Mother to Son

Well, son, I'll tell you:
Life for me ain't been no crystal stair.
It's had tacks in it,
And splinters,
And boards torn up,
And places with no carpet on the floor –
Bare.
But all the time
I'se been a-climbin' on,
And reachin' landin's,
And turnin' corners,
And sometimes goin' in the dark
Where there ain't been no light.
So, boy, don't you turn back.
Don't you set down on the steps
'Cause you find it's kinder hard.
Don't you fall now –
For I'se still goin', honey,
I'se still climbin',
And life for me ain't been no crystal stair.

Langston Hughes

The Most Important Rap

I am an astronaut
I circle the stars
I walk on the moon
I travel to Mars
I'm brave and tall
There is nothing I fear
And I am the most important person here.

I am a teacher
I taught you it all
I taught you why your
spaceship doesn't fall
If you couldn't read or write
Where would you be?
The most important person here is me.

Who are you kidding?
Are you taking the mick?
Who makes you better
when you're feeling sick?
I am a doctor
and I'm always on call
and I am more important than you all.

But I'm your mother
Don't forget me
If it wasn't for your mother
where would you be?
I washed your nappies
and changed your vest
I'm the most important
and mummy knows best.

I am a child
and the future I see
and there'd be no future
if it wasn't for me
I hold the safety
of the planet in my hand
I'm the most important
and you'd better understand.

Now just hold on
I've a message for you all
Together we stand
and divided we fall
So let's make a circle
And all remember this
Who's the most important?
Everybody is.
Who's the most important?
EVERYBODY IS!

Roger Stevens

The News

I don't like news
that explodes
leaves refugees
crying, homeless

that orders tanks
into cities
blasting down
schools and houses.

News that blows up
hospitals
news that kills
and fills deep graves.

I don't like news
that screams abuse
kicks the legs
from under wingers.

taps their ankles
argues back
news that won't learn
how to lose.

I like news
that's just been born
news that puts
food in stomachs.

news that rescues
news that cures
that celebrates
its hundredth birthday

news that will make today
happier than the day before.

David Harmer

Just One Wish (feeling full of joy)

If I had only one wish
I would drop it in a rippling pool
and watch the concentric circles
it would make as it plunged downwards
fragmenting the surface of the water.

If I had only one wish
I'd throw it high into the blue heaven
and watch it as it arched over
and tumbled down, creating
a rainbow of joy in the roof of the world.

If I had only one wish
I'd plant it deep in brown earth
and watch as it pierced the loam
with a pointed spear
and grew into a magnificent tree.

If I had only one wish
I'd burn it like incense
and savour the aroma as it wafted
far away on the winds of perfume
and dissipated on the thermals of life.

If I had only one wish
I should wish that everyone
could once again be filled with childlike joy
So that the magic and beauty of the world
would once again be a daily miracle.

Janis Priestley

Finding Magic

Are you looking for magic?
It's everywhere.
See how a kestrel
Hovers in air;
Watch a cat move:
What elegant grace!
See how a conker
Fits its case.
Watch a butterfly come
From a chrysalis,
Or a chick from an egg –
There's magic in this;
Then think of the
Marvellous mystery
Of an acorn becoming
A huge oak tree.
There's magic in sunsets
And patterned skies:
There's magic in moonlight –
Just use your eyes!
If you're looking for magic
It's easily found:
It's everywhere,
It's all around.

Eric Finney

With My Hands

Flap them in the air
    (wave)
Shove the ball away
    (save)
Smooth a doggie's fur
    (stroke)
Dig into a rib
    (poke).

Grasp another hand
    (shake)
Stick two bits of wood
    (make)
Squeeze an empty can
    (crunch)
Fingers in a fist
    (punch).

Slip a silver coin
    (pay)
Push them palm to palm
    (pray)
Test the water's heat
    (dip)
Hang on for your life
    (grip)

Push or pull a chair
   (shift)
Raise a weight up high
   (lift)
Press the button down
   (click)
Finger up your nose
   (pick)

Grab an arm or leg
   (catch)
Give an itch a bash
   (scratch)
Knock on someone's door
   (rap)
Thank you very much
   (clap)

Steve Turner

All of Us

All of us are afraid
More often than we tell.

There are times we cling like mussels to the sea wall,
And pray that the pounding waves
Won't smash our shell.

Times we hear nothing but the sound
Of our loneliness, like a cracked bell
From fields far away where the trees are in icy shade.

O many a time in the night-time and in the day,
More often than we say,
We are afraid.

If people say they are never frightened,
I don't believe them
If people say they are frightened,
I want to retrieve them.

From that dark shivering haunt
Where they don't want to be,
Nor I.

Let's make of ourselves, therefore, an enormous sky
Over whatever
We hold most dear.

And we'll comfort each other,
Comfort each other's
Fear.

Kit Wright

A School Creed

This is our school.
Let peace dwell here,
Let the room(s) be full of contentment,
Let love abide here,
Love of one another,
Love of mankind,
Love of life itself,
And love of God.
Let us remember
That, as many hands build a house,
So many hearts make a school.

Traditional (used by a school in Canada)

Listen

Listen.
Far away, the snort of a camel,
The swish of boots in the endless sand,
The whisper of silk and the clatter of ceremonial swords,
Far away.

Listen.
Not so far, the slam of a castle door,
A cry of rage on the midnight air,
A jangle of spurs and the cold thrust of a soldier's
    command,
Not so far.

Listen.
Closer now, the homely bleat of a ewe among the grasses,
The answering call of her lamb, fresh born,
The rattle of stones on a hillside path,
Closer now.

Listen.
Closer still, the murmur of women in the dark,
The kindly creak of a stable door,
The steady breathing of the sleepy beasts,
Closer still.

Listen.
So close you are almost there,
The singing of the stars,
The soundless flurry of wings,
The soft whimper of a child amongst the straw,
So close you are almost there.

Clare Bevan

Carol of the Brown King

Of the three Wise Men
Who came to the King,
One was a brown man,
So they sing.

Of the three Wise Men
Who followed the Star,
One was a brown king
From afar.

They brought fine gifts
Of spices and gold
In jewelled boxes
Of beauty untold.

Unto His humble
Manger they came
And bowed their heads
In Jesus' name.

Three Wise Men,
One dark like me –
Part of His
Nativity.

Langston Hughes

The Sky

The sky at night is like a big city
Where beast and men abound.
But never once has anyone
Killed a fowl or a goat,
And no bear has ever killed a prey.
There are no accidents: there are no losses.
Everything knows its way.

Traditional, Ewe (Ghana)

And My Heart Soars

The beauty of the trees,
the softness of the air,
the fragrance of the grass,
   speaks to me.

The summit of the mountain,
the thunder of the sky,
the rhythm of the sea,
   speaks to me.

The faintness of the stars,
the freshness of the morning,
the dew drop on the flower,
   speaks to me.

The strength of fire,
the taste of salmon,
the trail of the sun,
and the life that never goes away,
   they speak to me.

And my heart soars.

Chief Dan George

An Alphabet for the Planet

A for air.
The gentle breeze by which we live.
B for bread.
A food to bake, and take – and *give*.
C for climate.
It can be warm, it can be cold . . .
D for dolphin.
A smiling friend no net should hold.
E for Earth.
Our ship through space, and home to share.
F for family.
Which also means people *everywhere*.
G for green.
Colour of life we'll help to spread.
H for healthy.
Happy and strong, no fumes with lead.
I for ivory.
The elephant's tusks, his *own* to keep.
J for jungle.
A rainforest. No axe should creep.
K for kindly.
To everyone, gentle and good.
L for life.
It fills the sea and town and wood.

M for mother.
She may feel hurt, but loves us all.
N for nest.
A tiny home for chicks so small.
O for Ozone.
It shields our Earth from harmful rays.
P for peace.
'My happy dream,' the Planet says.
Q for quiet.
Where no loud noise can get at you.
R for recycled.
Old cans and cards as good as new.
S for Sun.
The nearest star. It gives us light.
T for tree.
A grander plant, a green delight.
U for united.
Working as one to put things right.
V for victory.
Winning over disease and war.
W for water.
The whole earth drinks when rainclouds pour.
X for Xylophone.
Music from wood – the high notes soar!
Y for yummy.
Those tasty fruits 'organically grown'.
Z for zoo.
A cage, a condor – sad, alone.

Riad Nourallah

Thank You Letter

Dear Sun,
Just a line to say:
Thanks for this
And every day.
Your dawns and sunsets
Are just great –
Bang on time,
Never late.
On dismal days,
As grey as slate,
Behind a cloud
You calmly wait,
Till out you sail
With cheerful grace
To put a smile
On the whole world's face.
Thanks for those

Blazing days on beaches.
For ripening apples,
Pears and peaches;
For sharing out
Your noble glow;
For sunsets – the
Loveliest things I know.
Please carry on:
We know your worth.

Love from
A Friend on Planet Earth

Eric Finney

Our Tree

It takes so long for a tree to grow
So many years of pushing the sky.

Long branches stretch their arms
Reach out with their wooden fingers.

Years drift by, fall like leaves
From green to yellow then back to green.

Since my grandad was a boy
And then before his father's father

There's been an elm outside our school
Its shadow long across our playground.

Today three men ripped it down.
Chopped it up. It took ten minutes.

David Harmer

Grown-ups

Where are your trainers and where is your coat
Where is your pen and where are your books
Where is the paper and where is the key
Where is the sugar and where is the tea
Where are your socks
Your bag and your hat?
Tidy your room!
Look after the cat!

You're hopeless
Untidy
You lose everything.

Where is your bracelet and where is your ring
Where is your ruler
Hymn book and shoes
Where is your scarf?
You lose and you lose.

You're hopeless
Untidy
You lose everything.

Careless and casual
You drop and you fling
You're destructive and thoughtless
You don't seem to care
Your coat's on the floor
Your boots on the chair

Why don't you think
Why don't you try
Learn to be helpful; like your father and I.

Mum . . . Dad . . .

Where are the woodlands, the corncrake and the whales
Where are all the dolphins, the tigers and dales
Where are the Indians, the buffalo herds
Fishes and forests and great flying birds

Where are the rivers
Where are the seas
Where are the marshes
And where are the trees

Where is the pure air
Acid-free showers
Where are the moorlands
The meadows and flowers?

These were your treasures
Your keepsakes of time
You've lost them
You've sold them
And they could have been mine.

Peter Dixon

The Last Day of School

I'm so glad it's finally over!
I've waited all year for this day!
It's ended, concluded and finished!
The one word for that is *hooray*!
So why am I getting this feeling
That maybe I'll miss everyone?
And why is there always some sadness
When everything's over and done?

Jeff Moss

Personal, Social and Sensitive Issues

Extract from the Book of Ecclesiastes

To every thing there is a season,
and a time to every purpose under heaven:
A time to be born, and a time to die;
a time to plant, and a time to pluck up that which is planted;
A time to kill, and a time to heal;
a time to break down, and a time to build up;
A time to weep, and a time to laugh;
a time to mourn, and a time to dance;
A time to cast away stones, and a time to gather stones together;
a time to embrace, and a time to refrain from embracing;
A time to get, and a time to lose;
a time to keep, and a time to cast away;
A time to rend, and a time to sew;
a time to keep silence, and a time to speak;
A time to love, and a time to hate;
a time of war, and a time of peace.

King James Bible

Name-calling

They called me frog-face with ears like a bat.
I said, 'I'm not – I'm worse than that.'

They called me rat-nose with a tongue like a shoe.
I said, 'Is that the best you can do?'

They called me mouse-eyes, skunk-breath, dog-head.
I said, 'I'm worse than all that you've said.'

They said, 'It's no fun calling you a name.'
I called, 'That's a pity – I'm enjoying this game.'

Charles Thomson

Give Yourself a Hug

Give yourself a hug
when you feel unloved

Give yourself a hug
when people put on airs
to make you feel a bug

Give yourself a hug
when everyone seems to give you
a cold-shoulder shrug

Give yourself a hug –
a big big hug

And keep on singing,
'Only one in a million like me
Only one in a million-billion-thrillion-zillion
like me.'

Grace Nichols

First Thing Today

(for Jimmy)

First thing today before
the cockerel crowed –
a baby's cry from
across the road.

Hi there, baby,
damp and furled,
hi there. Welcome
to our world.

Here's the little finger
of my right hand
and here's a teddy
you won't understand

                              yet

                                      and

here's

flowers for your mummy
and what about this? –
Here's my first hug
and my first kiss.

Fred Sedgwick

Some Things Don't Make Any Sense at All

My mum says I'm her sugarplum.
My mum says I'm her lamb.
My mum says I'm completely perfect
Just the way I am.
My mum says I'm a super-special wonderful terrific little guy.
My mum just had another baby.
Why?

Judith Viorst

Staring

out
the window
on the long ride
to
South Eighth Street School
on the
bursting
crowded
city bus

I wonder
if Daddy
ever –

even for a
little while –

thinks
about me –

thinks
about
us.

Lee Bennett Hopkins

It's Not the Same without Dad

I always sat on his knee
for the scary bits when we watched TV,
my head tucked into his chest.
Mum always fidgets, Dad was best.

And it's not the same without Dad.

He piggy-backed me up the stairs,
pulled sticky bubblegum out of my hair,
didn't tell Mum when he should have done,
when Dad played around it was really fun.

And it's not the same without Dad.

We fed the ducks down at the park,
he held me when I was scared of the dark,
he didn't mind if I got things wrong,
when I felt weak, he was sure to be strong.

But everything's changed now he's gone.

Brian Moses

Divorce

Dad's left.   Is that right?

Yes.
It all
centred
on something
Mum said.

So   does   leave

where   that   you?

Gina Douthwaite

Divorce

I did not promise
to stay with you till death us do part, or
anything like that,
so part I must, and quickly. There are things
I cannot suffer
any longer: Mother, you have never, ever, said
a kind word
or a thank you for all the tedious chores I have done;
Father, your breath
smells like a camel's and gives me the hump;
all you ever say is:
'Are you off in the cream puff, Lady Muck?'
In this day and age?
I would be better off in an orphanage.

I want a divorce.
There are parents in the world whose faces turn
up to the light
who speak in the soft murmur of rivers
and never shout.
There are parents who stroke their children's cheeks
in the dead night
and sing in the colourful voices of rainbows,
red to blue.
These parents are not you. I never chose you.
You are rough and wild,
I don't want to be your child. All you do is shout
and that's not right.
I will file for divorce in the morning at first light.

Jackie Kay

Bringing up a Single Parent

It's tough bringing up a single parent.
They get really annoyed when they can't stay out late,
or when you complain about them acting soppy
over some nerdy new friend,
(even though you are doing it for their own good).
It's exhausting sometimes, the way you have to please them,
and do things you absolutely hate while pretending
it's exactly what you want.
Yep. Bringing up a single parent
is a real chore.
You don't get extra pocket money for them,
or special grants,
and you have to get up in the morning
and allow them to take you to school
so they can boast to their friends
about how clever you are.
And what's worse,
you have to allow them to fret over you,
otherwise they get terribly worried.
And if you're out doing something interesting after school
you have to keep popping home all the time
to check they're not getting up to any mischief
with a new friend, or smoking, or drinking too much.
You have to try and give single parents
that extra bit of attention.
But once you've got them trained,
with a bit of patience and fortitude
they're relatively easy to look after.

Still, it can be tough
bringing up a single parent.

Brian Patten

Cousins

Every evening
when the dark creeps in
like a smothering black cape,
our little family
– Mum, Dad, Brother, Sister, Gogo the Cat and me –
we get together to huddle and cuddle
and keep us each safe.

Every night
when the moon rises like a white saucer,
our little family
– Mum, Dad, Brother, Sister, Gogo the Cat and me –
go to bed in our warm rooms.
We tuck each other in
and sleep safe in green dreams.

But in another land,
when the same dark creeps in,
a broken family in a wild wind
looks to the same moon, red and angry,
and each makes a wish.
– Mum, Dad, Brother, Sister, Asmara the Stray Dog –
all ask for food, for medicine, for peace, for rain.
Just these, only these, do our beautiful cousins ask for.

John Rice

Get Your Things Together, Hayley

Mum said the dreaded words this morning:
Get your things together, Hayley,
We're moving.

I've at last made a friend, and Mrs Gray
Has just stopped calling me
The New Girl.

Why do we have to go now
When I'm just beginning
To belong?

It's OK for my sister,
She's good with people.
They like her.

But I can't face the thought
Of starting all over again
In the wrong uniform.

Knowing the wrong things,
In a class full of strangers
Who've palled up already.

And don't need me.
Mum says: *It's character-forming, Hayley.*
I say it's terribly lonely.

Frances Nagle

The New House

I don't much like this bedroom
The bedroom doesn't like me
It looks like a sort of policeman
Inspecting a refugee.

I don't like the look of the bathroom
It's just an empty space
And the mirror seems used to staring at
A completely different face.

I don't like the smell of the kitchen
And the garden wet with rain
It feels like an empty station
Where I'm waiting for a train.

I can't kick a ball against this wall,
I can't build a house in this tree
And the streets are as quiet and deserted
As the local cemetery.

I don't like the look of the kids next door
Playing in the beat-up car
Why do they stand and stare at me?
Who do they think they are?

The big boy's coming over
He's just about my height
Why has he got a brick in his hand?
Is he going to pick a fight?

But he asks me into their garden
Tells me his name is Ben
And Jane is the name of his sister
And will I help build their den.

We can't get it finished by dinner
We won't get it finished by tea
But there's plenty of time in the days ahead
For Ben and for Jane and for me.

Gareth Owen

This Is a Recorded Message

Ring home, ring home . . .
She's punched her last coin in.
There's a pinball flicker of connections, then
The ansafone –

a so-familiar voice, slow,
strained, strange, like a brain-
washed hostage. *Please leave your name
and address. Please speak after the tone.*

Meeeee . . . bleats the ghost
in the machine that's waiting
in an empty house a hundred miles away. What can she say?
'This is me. I've left home.'

Philip Gross

Friends

When first I went to school
I walked with Sally.
She carried my lunch pack,
Told me about a book she'd read
With a handsome hero
So I said,
'You be my best friend.'
After break I went right off her.
I can't say why
And anyway I met Joan
Who's pretty with dark curls
And we sat in a corner of the playground
And giggled about the boy who brought the milk.
Joan upset me at lunch,
I can't remember what she said actually,
But I was definitely upset
And took up with Hilary
Who's frightfully brilliant and everything
And showed me her history
Which I considered very decent.
The trouble with Hilary is
She has to let you know how clever she is
And I said,
'You're not the only one who's clever you know,'
And she went all quiet and funny

And hasn't spoken to me since.
Good riddance I say
And anyway Linda is much more my type of girl;
She does my hair in plaits
And says how pretty I look,
She really says what she thinks
And I appreciate that.
Nadine said she was common
When we saw her on the bus that time
Sitting with three boys from that other school,
And I had to agree
There was something in what she said.
There's a difference between friendliness
And being cheap
And I thought it my duty
To tell her what I thought.
Well she laughed right in my face
And then pretended I wasn't there
So I went right off her.
If there's one thing I can't stand
It's being ignored and laughed at.
Nadine understood what I meant,
Understood right away
And that's jolly nice in a friend.

I must tell you one thing about her,
She's rather a snob.
I get the feeling
She looks down on me
And she'll never come to my house
Though I've asked her thousands of times.
I thought it best to have it out with her
And she went off in a huff
Which rather proved my point
And I considered myself well rid.

At the moment
I walk home on my own
But I'm keeping my eyes open
And when I see somebody I consider suitable
I'll befriend her.

Gareth Owen

Friendship

Friendship
Is precious
Keep it
Protect it
You will need it
Don't throw it away
Don't break it
Don't neglect it
Keep it
Somewhere
In your heart
If you want to
Somewhere in your thoughts
If you want to
But keep it
For, friendship

Has no borders
And its boundary
Is that of the world
It is the colour
Of the rainbow
And it has the beauty
Of a dream
Never listen
To those who say
It doesn't exist any more
It is here
It is yours
When you want it
All you have to do is:
Open
Your eyes

Véronique Tadjo (Côte d'Ivoire)

Friends

I fear it's very wrong of me
And yet I must admit
When someone offers friendship
I want the *whole* of it.
I don't want everybody else
To share my friends with me.
At least, I want *one* special one,
Who, indisputably
   Likes me much more than all the rest,
Who's always on my side.
Who never cares what others say,
Who lets me come and hide
Within his shadow, in his house –
It doesn't matter where –
Who lets me simply be myself, ·
Who's always, *always* there.

Elizabeth Jennings

Harvey

Harvey doesn't laugh about how I stay short while
   everybody grows.
Harvey remembers I like jellybeans – except black.
Harvey lends me shirts I don't have to give back.
I'm scared of ghosts and only Harvey knows.

Harvey thinks I will when I say someday I will marry
   Margie Rose.
Harvey shares his lemonade – sip for sip.
He whispers 'zip' when I forget to zip.
He swears I don't have funny looking toes

Harvey calls me up when I'm in bed with a sore throat and
   runny nose.
Harvey says I'm nice – but not *too* nice.
And if there's a train to Paradise.
I won't get on it unless Harvey goes.

Judith Viorst

Dream Team

My team
Will have all the people in it
Who're normally picked last.

Such as me.

When it's my turn to be chooser
I'll overlook Nick Magic-Feet-Jones
And Supersonic Simon Hughes

And I'll point at my best friend Sean
Who'll faint with surprise
And delight.

And at Robin who's always the one
Left at the end that no one chose –
Unless he's away, in which case it's guess who?

And Tim who can't see a thing
Without his glasses.
I'll pick him.

And the rest of the guys that Mr Miller
Calls dead-legs but only need their chance
To show what they're made of.

We'll play in the cup final
In front of the class, the school, the town,
The world, the galaxy.

And due to the masterly leadership shown
By their captain, not forgetting
His three out-of-this-world goals,

We'll WIN.

Frances Nagle

New Girl

Have you seen the new girl?
    first-day-at-our-school girl
    not-sure-what-to-do girl
    no-partner-in-the-queue girl
    mouth-stuck-down-like-glue girl
    looking-a-little-blue girl
    needs-a-friend-or-two girl
So what are you going to *do* girl?

Danielle Sensier

Shame

There's a girl at school
we teased today;
made jokes, called her names.
My friends all laughed,
called it harmless fun,
said it was just a game.

Now I'm at home
feeling horrid inside,
long gone that thoughtless grin.
How will I face her
tomorrow at school?
I wish I hadn't joined in.

Tracey Blance

Bullied

Bullies get you.
I don't know how but they do.
They seem to have some
secret inborn radar
tuned in to loners,
quiet ones,
different ones.

You don't have to
do anything, say anything.
Seems you just have to be you.

Grown-ups think they know.
Bullies? Just cowards, they say,
unsure of themselves,
needing to act big.
But it's hard to believe
when jeering faces
zoom up to yours.

When they're hassling you,
calling you names,
leading the chanting,
the whispering,
urging the others on,
a relentless horde
of nagging, pecking birds.

Then there's the 'in-betweens',
the waiting, the not knowing,
just sure that
sooner or later
it's going to come.
The worst times;
the thinking times.

Don't ask me the answer.
I don't know but –
I'm getting there.

Keep my eyes skinned,
find a crowd to vanish into
before *they* see *me*.
Cornered, I know I can't look them
in the eye – but I've learned
not to look at the floor,
to try and walk tall.

Mostly I've learned
to talk in my head,
tell myself
it's not me, I'm all right –
they're the idiots, the misfits.
Eventually
it begins to sink in.

I'm getting tougher inside.
It's working.
Just don't give in.

Try anything, anything.
But don't *let* them win.

Patricia Leighton

Sometimes

(A cinquain)

Sometimes
They just stare hard
Nudge each other and smile,
And I pretend that I don't care –
Sometimes

Coral Rumble

Dobbo's First Swimming Lesson

Dobbo's fists
spiked me to the playground wall
nailed me to the railings.

The plastic ball
he kicked against my skinny legs
on winter playtimes

Bounced a stinging red-hot bruise
across the icy tarmac.

The day we started swimming
we all jumped in
laughed and splashed, sank beneath
the funny tasting water.

Shivering in a corner
Dobbo crouched, stuck to the side
sobbing like my baby brother
when all the lights go out.

David Harmer

It Hurts

It hurts when someone makes remarks
About the clothes I wear,
About the foods I refuse to eat
Or the way I cover my hair.

It hurts when someone laughs and jokes
About the way I speak.
'Ignore them,' says my dad, but it's hard
To turn the other cheek.

It hurts when someone calls me names
Because of the colour of my skin.
Everyone's different outside
But we're all the same within.

John Foster

Mr Mizen

Mr Mizen fell in the street.
Old and frail, his step was unsure on the ice.
No one saw him fall
but the cry of the concrete shook the town.

A passing runner stopped to help.
But strong as he was
he had no understanding of old age,
the slowness it brings, how the wind
tangles weak limbs, how hard it is
to heave tired legs over uneven pavement slabs.

After falling Mr Mizen had no idea
what had happened to him.
He asked if his pipe was broken,
he fumbled for his glasses
and asked if he could go home.

'Is there someone at home
who'll look after you?'
'No, I'm on my own.'

No wife, no son, no daughter
to wipe his bleeding chin,
to put him to bed,
to make him some soup,
to see that he recovered.

So when Mr Mizen fell in the street
the authorities decided he couldn't go home
but that he should go to hospital,
to be another number.

A week later the local newspaper
reported that he had 'died of natural causes'.

But, being as alone as he was,
is not what you'd call 'natural'.

John Rice

On the Streets

Welcome to Cardboard City
No windows, doors, or locks
All you need is a sleeping bag
All you need is a box.

It starts with a row at home
A rumble, a hassle, a fight
Your mum and dad chuck you out
And you've got no bed for the night.

You can beg for a bit of money
Spend it on beer and draw
Just watch out for the boots and knives
And the steady beat of the Law.

You've joined the homeless people
Dropped here until you rot
No one much cares if you live or die
You're the one everybody forgot.

David Harmer

My Daddy Dances Tapstep

Roger's daddy's clever
Daisy's flies a plane
Michael does computers
And has a house in Spain.
Lucy's goes to London
He stays there every week . . .
   But my daddy has an earring
      and lovely dancing feet.

He hasn't got a briefcase
He hasn't got a phone
He hasn't got a mortgage
And we haven't got a home.
He hasn't got a fax machine
We haven't got a car
   But he can dance and fiddle
      And my daddy is
      A Star.

                              Peter Dixon

The World Is a Beautiful Place

The world is a beautiful place
                to be born into
if you don't mind happiness
                not always being
                          so very much fun
if you don't mind a touch of hell
                now and then
        just when everything is fine
                        because even in heaven
                they don't sing
                        all the time
        The world is a beautiful place
                        to be born into
if you don't mind some people dying
                all the time
        or maybe only starving
                        some of the time
                which isn't half so bad
                                if it isn't you.

Laurence Ferlinghetti

In the Garden

There's a plant in the garden with white flowers
And a plant in the garden with blue,
Which of them is better?
Neither one said Sue.

There's a plant in the garden with cream flowers
And a plant in the garden with red,
Which of them is better?
Neither Simon said.

Those plants in the garden so tiny
And those trees in the garden so tall,
Which of them is better?
Neither answered Paul . . .
The garden needs them all.

Philip Waddell

Citizen of the World

when you are very small
maybe not quite born
your parents move
for some reason you may never understand they move
from their own town
from their own land
and you grow up in a place
that is never quite your home

and all your childhood people
with a smile or a fist say
you're not from here are you
and part of you says fiercely yes I am
and part of you feels no I'm not
I belong where my parents belonged

but when you go to their town, their country
people there also say
you're not from here are you
and part of you says no I'm not
and part of you feels fiercely yes I am

and so you grow up both and neither
and belong everywhere and nowhere much the same
both stronger and weaker for the lack of ground
able to fly but not to rest

339

and all over the world, though you feel alone
are millions like you, like a great flock of swallows
soaring or falling exhausted, wings beating the rhythm
of the wind that laughs at fences or frontiers,
whose home is itself, and the whole world it moves over.

Dave Calder

The Soldiers Came

The soldiers came
and dropped their bombs.
The soldiers didn't take long
to bring the forest down.

With the forest gone
the birds are gone.
With the birds gone
who will sing their song?

But the soldiers forgot
to take the forest
out of the people's hearts.
The soldiers forgot
to take the birds
out of the people's dreams.
And in the people's dreams
the birds still sing their song.

Now the children
are planting seedlings
to help the forest grow again.
they eat a simple meal of soft rice
wrapped in a banana leaf.
And the land welcomes their smiling
like a shower of rain.

John Agard

Stranger

You looked so sad when you came to us,
From a land so faraway.
You left your friends, your favourite foods,
The language that you spoke so well.
But you came to us with a lovely smile,
A beautiful dress, and a small soft voice,
Sometimes I know you felt so lost,
In the street of unfriendly noise.
And your mother smiled too,
She couldn't say much.
But I didn't need words to speak to you,
I knew from your smile
And the touch of your hand,
That we wouldn't be strangers
. . . for long.

Les Baynton

Arturi's Story

Arturi's skin is sort of grey,
grubby looking, know what I mean?
Miss Hampton says his country is at war
so he didn't get very good food before.
He's very quiet, doesn't talk much
about the things he saw
in his war.
I've never seen him laugh.
He hardly even smiles
but he often cries.
Our teacher tries to comfort him
with soothing words,
a warm hand on his shoulder,
a troubled look in her eyes.
Arturi's mother brought him here
to her sister's home.
His father is still there.
Arturi and his mum are not sure where.
Funny, I never took much notice
of the TV news until now.
Unreal, somehow.
These days in every scene
of buildings ripped apart
by banging shells,
seeing women duck and run,
a soldier at a corner
aiming a gun,
I think maybe Arturi's father is one
of the people caught up in that.

In the playground the other day
Tim and I were talking about the shops
on the way to school;
the green off-licence,
sweets in the post office
and how the smell
of fish and chips makes us drool.
Arturi was listening, hanging his head
the corners of his mouth turned down.
'My school was up in the mountains,'
he suddenly said.
That caught our attention right away.
We waited to hear what else
he might have to say.
'I had to get up
and eat breakfast in the night
because we had to be
at school in daytime,
there was no electric light.
My friend Thomas and I
we didn't like walking
up the mountain track in the dark
for two hours every day.
Spiders' webs hung on wet bushes.

The gloomy trees were spooky and grey.
Our voices echoed,
they startled us, sounding so loud.
We were frightened there might be
soldiers somewhere near
who would take us away.
The worst place on the way
was the rushing stream,
it was so fast and wide
with slippery wet stones
to balance and jump along
to reach the other side.
When our feet got wet
they were freezing cold all day.
Our school was just one big room
with a leaking roof,
no glass in the windows, no door,
a floor of muddy clay.
In the middle the old iron stove
stood, burning hot,
giving off fumes and smoke.
If you sat near enough
you warmed up a bit
but the fumes made you cough and choke.
Outside we'd piled rocks
halfway up the gaping window holes
to keep out the wind and cold.
We had a few wooden desks
with benches, all scored
with scratches, really old.'

Tim and I stand silent,
shuffle our feet.
'You must be glad to be here now,'
blurts Tim. I see he feels like me
as our eyes meet.
'Yes, but my best friend Tomas
is still doing that every day
up the mountain all alone,' Arturi groans.
We can see from the way
he swallows and rubs an eye
he's trying not to cry.
'What about . . . well,
why don't you write him a letter
asking, "Are you OK?"
Here Arturi. Have a sweet,' I awkwardly say.
And Tim and I resolve
Arturi deserves new friends
remembering Tomas
alone on the mountain
every day
that way.

Penny Kent

All that Space

Great-grandad
used to tell me stories,
tales about when he was a lad,

fled city streets,
flew on his bike
down lanes between cornfields,
past Kenyon's Brick Works
to the Moss,

sitting for hours
in all that space,

played his mouth organ,
and watched . . .
peewits   wild violets   silhouette
of chimneys against the sky,

his shabby jersey, battered clogs,
livened by new-moon-silver buds of willow,
baby-skin softness of dog-rose petal.

In the Home, people try to interest him
in television, don't understand
when he turns his chair to the wall
– the print of Constable's *Haywain*,
curves his fingers round
his smiling mouth,
and tilts his head, listening . . .

sitting for hours   in all that space.

Joan Poulson

Cowboy Games and the Good Death

In cowboy games we tumbled and cried in deaths so good
 that we got up and died all over again.
In those days death was often a matter for negotiation
 between killer and killed.
'You're dead.'
'Missed.'
'You aren't taking it.'
'It went under my arm.'
'You're out the game then.'
'OK. You got me. But I'm just knocked out.'
I dropped to the floor,
Held my arm
Shook my head
Staggered to my feet
Free to enjoy
A whole playtime of deaths.

Nan didn't fall down when she died
Because she was in hospital
Held down by blankets and tubes.
She didn't argue
She took it
And died just the once.

John Coldwell

The Funeral

Everyone is silent in the huge black car.
A cloud full of swallowed tears
gliding two feet above the ground
towards a storm.

We're trying to be brave.
Mum holds my hand tightly.
Her fingers are like clothes pegs
clinging to washing
in a force 9 gale.
'You're hurting me,' I say.
She lets me go –
a forgotten balloon
and smiles a smile from far away,
like a smile in a photograph
in a place you can't quite remember.

We wait in line.
People mumble past us
trying not to catch our eyes.
I look at the coffin
and try to imagine Granny inside.
Can she hear me singing?
I'm singing really loudly so she'll hear.

Is she in heaven yet?
Still old and in pain?
Or whirring swiftly backwards
like a rewound tape
which pauses
at your very favourite bit.

Are hosts of heavenly angels
even as we sing
loosening her tight grey perm
and itchy curls?
Making the hair flow
like a coppery stream
down her strong young back.

I wonder if she'll wear
her tartan slippers
to dance on the clouds.

Afterwards, outside,
we weave through furious rain
towards the car.
Inside and warm again,
Mum sighs
Like summer
drifting through an open window
A feather
      or a present
          from a sky-blue
              sky.

Lindsay MacRae

Mid-Term Break

I sat all morning in the college sick bay
Counting bells knelling classes to a close.
At two o'clock our neighbours drove me home.

In the porch I met my father crying –
He had always taken funerals in his stride –
And Big Jim Evans saying it was a hard blow.

The baby cooed and laughed and rocked the pram
When I came in, and I was embarrassed
By old men standing up to shake my hand

And tell me they were 'sorry for my trouble';
Whispers informed strangers I was the eldest,
Away at school, as my mother held my hand

In hers and coughed out angry tearless sighs.
At ten o'clock the ambulance arrived
With the corpse, stanched and bandaged by the nurses.

Next morning I went up into the room. Snowdrops
And candles soothed the bedside; I saw him
For the first time in six weeks. Paler now,

Wearing a poppy bruise on his left temple,
He lay in the four foot box as in his cot.
No gaudy scars, the bumper knocked him clear.

A four foot box, a foot for every year.

Seamus Heaney

My First Dog

Prince was my dog,
no one else's.
I couldn't remember a time
     when he wasn't there.

We grew up together,
roamed together,
got into trouble together,
winked at each other
and took our tellings-off
together.

He was my black-and-tan shadow,
sleeking along at my heels
tongue out,
chasing down the green hill
and the alleyway
to the corner shop.

He was my talisman;
with him I was safe.
He was my freedom,
his soft coat the cushion
of my dreams as I lay
tracing cloud
                patterns
                    in
                        the
                    sky.

And when he gashed his leg
on a rusted railing,
when my mother quietly told me
he had been put down,
he was the first black hole
of my young life.

The loneliness
of empty arms
and no warm neck
to put them round.

Patricia Leighton

Burying the Dog in the Garden

When we buried
the dog in
the garden on
the grave we put
a cross and
the tall man
next door was
cross.
'Animals have no
souls,' he said.
'They must have animals'
souls,' we said. 'No,'
he said and
shook his head.
'Do you need a
soul to go
to Heaven?' we
asked. He nodded
his head. 'Yes,'
he said.

'That means my
hamster's not
in Heaven,' said
Kevin. 'Nor is
my dog,' I said.
'My cat could sneak
in anywhere,' said
Clare. And we thought
what a strange place Heaven
must be with
nothing to stroke
for eternity.
We were all
seven.
We decided we
did not want to
go to Heaven.
For that the
tall man next
door is to blame.

Brian Patten

Silver Moon

When Amelia looks on the silver moon
She remembers her mother's smile,
The warmth of her arms around her,
The breeze of her breath on her brow,
And she wants her here with her now.

When Amelia looks on the silver moon
She forgets the many times
Her rebel ways or cheekiness
Made her mother frown,
And she wants her here with her now.

From beyond the moon, beyond the stars,
Beyond the deep, deep sky,
Her mother calls to her each night
'Amelia, I am here.'
And she calls back 'So am I.'

Frances Nagle

Death

There is no needle without piercing point.
There is no razor without trenchant blade.
Death comes to us in many forms.

With our feet we walk the goat's earth.
With our hands we touch God's sky.
Some future day in the heat of noon,
I shall be carried shoulder high
Through the village of the dead.
When I die, don't bury me under forest trees,
I fear their thorns.
When I die, don't bury me under forest trees,
I fear the dripping water.
Bury me under the great shade trees in the market,
I want to hear the drums beating
I want to feel the dancers' feet.

Kuba (Africa)

Remember

Remember me when I am gone away,
   Gone far away into the silent land;
   When you can no more hold me by the hand,
Nor I half turn to go yet turning stay.
Remember me when no more day by day
   You tell me of our future that you plann'd:
   Only remember me; you understand
It will be late to counsel then or pray.
Yet if you should forget me for a while
   And afterwards remember, do not grieve:
   For if the darkness and corruption leave
   A vestige of the thoughts that once I had,
Better by far you should forget and smile
   Than that you should remember and be sad.

Christina Rossetti

The
Environment

Wilderness

Miss says wilderness
is beautiful, natural, endless . . .
is space.

Mum's *Oxford English Dictionary* states:
'wild or uncultivated land'.

At the end of our garden
there's a lime tree.
I climb it, high as I can.

Sometimes
I sit up there for hours,
especially in the dark
staring at the stars,
touching wilderness,

out there
and inside me.

Joan Poulson

Web of Life

An invisible web,
as fragile as dreams,
links mountains to forests
and rivers to streams.

Through woodlands and forests;
where seas flow and ebb,
over ice caps and deserts,
life weaves a great web.

From plankton to whales,
all life great and small
depends on each other.
Life's web links us all.

And we must take care
of each gossamer thread,
for we are all part of
this great world wide web.

Jane Clarke

Dolphin Dance

We are darters and divers
from secret sea-caves.
We're dippers and gliders,
we dance through the waves.

We spiral and curl,
we weave as we fly,
stitch shimmering arches
from ocean to sky.

Judith Nicholls

Forest

The forest stretches for miles,
a place where labourers
poached rabbit for the pot,
where deer roamed free.
An ancient place, root and tree
firmly established,
majestic oaks spreading
into an eternity of time.

Still those oaks, now shedding
tough brown leaves, are here.
The forest floor rustles
with the sound of leaf
upon leaf of history.
Oak and birch set new seed,
regenerate themselves,
and slender saplings rise.

The forest is evolving, ever-
changing, yet the same.
Belonging to itself, never
planted, never tame.
Let this wish be granted:
that the forest will remain.

Ann Bonner

Natural Numbers

*Example: Divide 5,000 buffaloes
by fifty hunters = almost nothing left.*

1. Divide 200 elephants
by seventeen ivory poachers =

2. Divide two rainforests
by eight logging companies =

3. Divide one beautiful planet
by one greedy species =

Mike Johnson

Blake's Tyger – Revisited

*On hearing that tigers in captivity can gradually
lose their colour, losing their camouflaging stripes
and fading gradually to white.*

Tiger! Tiger! Turning white
In a cage just twice your height
Six paces left, six paces right,
A long slow day, a longer night.

Tiger! Tiger! Dreaming still
Of the scent? The chase? The kill?
And now? No need. No place. No scope.
No space. No point. No hope.

Tiger! Tiger! Paces. Paces.
Once he flashed through open spaces.
His world once echoed to his roars.
Now he's quiet. He stares. He snores.

An inch of sky glimpsed through the bars.
A puddle. Concrete. Smells of cars.
He sniffs the air. He slumps. He sighs.
And stares and stares through jaundiced eyes.

Michaela Morgan

The Last Wolf Speaks from the Zoo

By day

I hid in the ferns
pressed to the earth,
dressed in a coat
brown as turf.

Sunlight warmed
the patches where
my wolf pack once lay.

Day after day
childflesh spills past the wire;
they pause, point and stare –
I size them up –
glare back –
through thin red eyes.

Years back
my sister caught one –
cracked a finger –
left the childflesh
to scowl and howl.

The next day
they took my sister away.
But her smell stayed
trapped in the earth's spoor.
It took a full moon's span
for it to fade.

Now, alone,
I watch
and wait for her.

At night
the stars glisten.
I listen for the pack.
I sing to the moon.
I croon an ancient tune.
But she is muzzled
and cannot answer back.

Pie Corbett

Important Notice

World Wildlife Industries sadly announces
that we may soon have to close due to fierce
competition from Human Beings International.

Many of our famous products are already
unavailable including, to name but three, our dodo,
quagga and once healthy passenger pigeon lines.

Currently under threat are many of our
ancient stock of mammals and fishes as well as
birds, reptiles, amphibians *and* insects.

But even now we could be helped to survive.
Work together with your parents and teachers
to find out how you could all help before it is too late.

And remember – without us and the products
of our other branch, World Vegetation Industries,
our world too might soon be without *your* company.

Let's work together to stay in business.

Mother Nature

Managing Director

Philip Waddell

Names

My name is 'Couldn't care less',
just let the forests die.
My name is 'Can't be bothered',
who cares about holes in the sky?

My name is 'I'm too busy',
let someone else do the worrying,
there's nothing that I can do
if the ice caps are wearing thin.

My name is 'Leave me alone',
just don't go preaching to me.
Gossip is what I care about
not oil that's spilt in the sea.

My name is 'I'm all right Jack',
there's really no cause for alarm.
Hens are silly birds, who cares
if they suffer at the factory farm?

Who cares about global warming?
I like a spot of hot weather.
My name is 'Sit on the fence',
my name is 'All of a dither'.

So stop saying what I should think,
I don't want to believe what I'm told.
My name is 'Hope it will go away',
my name is 'Don't get involved'.

And who do you think you are,
telling us all we should worry?
WELL, MY NAME'S A WARNING FROM FUTURE YEARS,
IT'S 'LISTEN OR YOU'LL BE SORRY'.

Brian Moses

Dragonflies

They used to fly
over all the ponds
in summer, Granny says

like sparkling sapphire helicopters,
purple aeroplanes,
with eyes of bright topaz,
wings flashing emerald light,
brightening the countryside
in their jewelled flight.

Sun-glow brilliance winging
over every pond,
someday I hope to see one
– smallest last dragon.

Joan Poulson

Missing

Missing: our
one and only planet,
known to her friends as
'Earth'.

Yes, an old photograph
when she was clothed in
gorgeous greens,
wilderness white,
brilliant blues.

Somehow, got into
bad company:
blistered brown,
gaunt grey,
faded. Jaded,

left one morning;
no forwarding address.

We just didn't think . . .
We just didn't know . . .
what to do.

If you
have any information
that can help us trace
our beautiful planet,
please get in touch.

Please get in touch.

Mike Johnson

Model
Poems

Introduction

This section provides a broad range of poems that could be used as models for the children's own writing. Do not worry too much if the children find it difficult to adhere strictly to a form – concentrate on the quality of the language. Encourage them to use the poet's toolkit of techniques: precise nouns, powerful verbs, necessary adjectives, exact detail, contrasting and surprising combinations, alliteration, similes, metaphor, personification.

- 'Poetry' – make a list of rhyming couplets, using the same form, e.g. *Not the rain,/but the cool touch of rain;/Not the lion,/but the lion's mane,* etc.
- 'Alien Lullaby – either use the same structure (or base own poem on another well-known rhyme), e.g. *Hush little Hobbit, don't you cry!/Momma's gonna give you a plane to fly./and if that plane's wings should break/Momma's gonna take you to the lake . . .*
- 'Jabbermockery'/'Jabberwocky' and 'The Cook and the Caretaker'/'The Owl and the Pussy Cat' – further examples of poems based on the structure of an original.
- 'Song Thrush Poster' – poem in another form (other possibilities include diary, letters, for sale notices, phone conversations, etc.).
- 'Tom Thumb's Diary' – a good example of responding to a well-known rhyme or fairy tale, in another form – diary, letter, news item, for instance.
- 'There was a young lady . . .' – limericks are not an easy form. Rhyming dictionaries do help! When writing,

children should say the poem aloud to listen for the rhythm/beat.

- 'Low Owl' – this is a poem that only uses one of the five vowels (in this case the letter 'o'). Begin by trying to write sentences with only one vowel, e.g. *An ant can walk and talk*.
- 'Haiku of the Four Winds' – pupils could use the same format to write a similar haiku based on the sun, moon, rain, wind, thunder, etc. Note that the haiku do not have to stick strictly to 5/7/5 syllables but should aim to capture the essence of a scene in a few words. Begin by choosing a season to describe – list typical sights and sounds. Use this brainstorm as a basis for the poem. Short forms such as haiku lend themselves to writing a cycle of linked poems, such as a calendar of haiku.
- 'The Emperor and the Nightingale' – these three haiku keep to a strict pattern. They are connected and form a poem – called a rensaku.
- 'Tanka' – tease out the syllabic pattern (5/7/5/7/7). Note how like the haiku this is a verbal snapshot, related to one of the seasons.
- 'Cinquain' – again, let children work out the pattern (5 lines – 2/4/6/8/2 syllables). Imitate by selecting a month, listing sights and sounds and then using this list to construct a cinquain. Concentrate more on the quality of the words than fitting the pattern exactly.
- 'Kennings' – a Nordic form of poetry. Like a riddle the poem describes something in different ways. Choose something simple like a cat or dog and try a class example, e.g. *flea carrier/loud growler/ankle biter . . .*

- 'Two Witches Discuss . . .' – writing simple conversations between two characters can form the basis of a poem. Try well-known story characters, e.g. Jack meeting the giant.
- 'In Marble Walls' – see who can work out the riddle. Give this several days if need be. As a class choose a subject, e.g. a candle. List all that is known about the subject and turn these into clues – as in 'What am I?'
- 'One line riddles' – give these as homework – who can work out what they are? Select subjects and offer one clue only.
- 'My First Is in Two . . .' – tease out from the spelling the answer to this riddle. Use it as a basis for class riddles written in the same style.
- 'A Pin Has a Head' – list other words that have several meanings (*watch, wave, crane, rose, ring, club, bank, light, pop, tug, stand, book, leaves, flat, safe, jam, arms, bat*) and let children invent similar sentences, perhaps as one line 'word plays', e.g. *A watch has hands but no fingers.*
- 'What Am I?' – to make a simple riddle take a common subject (mirror, windows, lock, etc.). Brainstorm associations (*mirror – glass, reflections, thin, cannot lie, seven years' bad luck, 'mirror, mirror on the wall'*, etc.). Create a poem by listing clues, e.g. *I am made of glass/and reflect all that I see./I seem to hold the world/and yet I am empty./Drop me – and you'll/have seven years' bad luck . . . etc.*
- 'The Tree Spell' – what about using the same format for an animal such as a badger which hibernates?
- 'The Months' – write a simple poem in which you use one or two lines to describe what happens in each month, e.g. *January is snow bound./In February icicles hang from the roof . . .*

- 'Apple Pie' – choose a different subject and use the same pattern. For instance, a poem based on a pencil might start – *A altered it, B bit it, C cracked it in half, D dug it into a table top, E elongated it . . .*
- 'Simple Seasons' – these acrostics look easy but are difficult to write effectively. Try writing some based on months rather than seasons, e.g.

  Dull,

  Early nights.

  Christmas lights gleam.

  Empty streets, sirens scream.

  Misty windows.

  Baubles like tiny planets.

  Enticing shop displays.

  Rough winds and frosted days.
- 'The Witch, the Prince and the Girl in the Tower' – an interesting concrete poem. The shape adds to the meaning – it is twisted in a plait. Try writing another thin poem where two characters speak to each other in the same sort of format. What might Jack say and the Giant reply? Keep it to just one sentence each. Do not worry too much about rhyme as this so often gets in the way of the quality of the writing.
- 'Litter Lout' – another shape poem where the pattern visually represents the meaning. Make a list of similes for the snow – using 'like' and 'as' (as cold as . . .). List what else snow does – how does it fall, how does it lie, how does it feel, what does it remind you of, etc. Use these ideas to create a similar shape poem.
- 'My Dad's Amazing' – make a list of other idioms and try the same sort of idea.

- 'Things to Do' – other possibilities would include – things to do on holiday, at the beach, in the park, after school, at a party.
- 'Moses' – invent other tongue-twisters by using words that alliterate and rhyme.
- 'Childhood Tracks' – this poem uses the senses and a simple format. Copy it, brainstorming ideas and basing it firmly in the children's own lives and memories.
- 'Mr Khan's Shop' – write a list poem based on foods that we eat – the variety is surprising, e.g. *In my mum's kitchen cupboard/there are round potatoes, slim courgettes,/orange onions with peeling skin,/violet bulbs of garlic . . .*
- 'What Do You Collect?' – a straightforward imitation of this poem would be possible to write rhyming couplets. The rhyme may be hard and children should abandon words if sensible rhymes cannot be found. Writing in pairs can work well for this sort of task.
- 'Bonfire Night' – rather like a haiku, this simple, short poem makes a useful model. Select a special event, such as a visit to the seaside. Let pupils take one sense impression, and see if they can write a short poem concentrating on selecting powerful language, e.g. *Taste of ice cream/frozen crystals – the sun glares down/melting the crisp edges.*
- 'Notes towards a Poem' – use the phrase 'inside my head' to write a list poem of all the things that might be inside the mind – memories, fears, wishes, dreams, etc. Compare this poem to Miroslav Holub's poem 'A Boy's Head' and Katherine Gallagher's poem 'A Girl's Head', both found in *Ramshackle Rainbow, Poems for Year 5*, edited by Pie Corbett (Macmillan Children's Books).

- 'A Minute to Midnight' – imitate this contrasting list poem by listing all the things that are still or moving at a given time of day. Try adding in more description.
- 'Best Places' – list favourite places, objects, memories, events and use the same sort of pattern to create individual list poems.
- 'The Dream Keeper' – use the repeating phrase 'bring me all of your . . .' to write a similar poem. This could include memories, hopes, wishes, etc.
- 'Dreams' – use this poem as a basic pattern to create a list poem using metaphors, e.g. Hold fast to dreams/ for if dreams live/ Life would be a red racing car/ whispering the motorway.
- 'All the world's a stage . . .' – use this poem as a basis to trigger writing, listing all the things on the world's stage that we enjoy, e.g. *On the world's stage/ I see the sea rippling in the blue./ I see the football smack into the net./ I see . . . etc.*
- 'Camilla Caterpillar' etc – children love tongue-twisters and playing with alliteration. Write simple tongue-twisters about animals by seeing how many words can be used that share the same opening sound, e.g. cat – *the curious cat crept carefully, concealing a clammy cod!*
- 'Having My Ears Boxed' – look at how the poem is built around the possible different meanings of 'having my ears boxed' – a pun. Look at other words that might mean several different things, e.g. *bat, watch, wave*. 'A Pin Has No Head' is another poem that involves this sort of word play.

Poetry

What is Poetry? Who Knows?
Not a rose, but the scent of the rose;
Not the sky, but the light in the sky;
Not the fly, but the gleam of the fly;
Not the sea, but the sound of the sea;
Not myself, but what makes me
See, hear, and feel something that prose
Cannot: and what it is, who knows?

Eleanor Farjeon

Alien Lullaby

Hush, little alien, don't you cry!
Mamma's gonna bake you a moonbeam pie

And if that moonbeam pie goes stale
Mamma's gonna catch you a comet's tail

And if that comet's tail won't flip
Mamma's gonna make you a rocket ship

And if that rocket ship won't stay
Mamma's gonna buy you the Milky Way

And if the Milky Way's too far
Mamma's gonna bring you a shooting star

And if that shooting star falls down –
You're still the sweetest little alien in town!

Sue Cowling

Jabberwocky

'Twas brillig, and slithy toves
Did gyre and gimble in the wabe;
All mimsy were the borogoves,
And the mome raths outgrabe.

'Beware the Jabberwock, my son!
The jaws that bite, the claws that catch!
Beware the Jubjub bird, and shun
The frumious Bandersnatch!'

He took his vorpal sword in hand:
Long time the manxome foe he sought –
So rested he by the Tumtum tree,
And stood awhile in thought.

And as in uffish thought he stood,
The Jabberwock, with eyes of flame,
Came whiffling through the tulgey wood
And burbled as it came!

One, two! One, two! And through and through
The vorpal blade went snicker-snack!
He left it dead, and with its head
He went galumphing back.

'And hast thou slain the Jabberwock?
Come to my arms, my beamish boy!
O frabjous day! Callooh! Callay!'
He chortled in his joy.

'Twas brillig, and the slithy toves
Did gyre and gimble in the wabe;
All mimsy were the borogoves,
And the mome raths outgrabe.

Lewis Carroll

Jabbermockery

Twas Thursday and the bottom set
Did gyre and gimble in the gym.
All mimsy was Miss Borogrove
And the Head of Maths was grim.

'Beware the Mathematix, my friend!
His sums that snarl. His coordinates that catch!
Beware the Deputy Bird, and shun
The evil Earring-snatch!'

She took her ballpoint pen in hand:
Long time the problem's end she sought –
So rested she by the lavatory
And sat awhile in thought.

And as in toughish thought she sat,
The Mathematix with eyes of flame
Came calculating through the cloakroom doors
And subtracted as he came.

She thought real fast as he went past;
The well placed soap went slickersmack!
She left him stunned and with the sums
She went galumphing back.

'And hast thou got the answers, Jackie?
Come to our desk,' beamed idle boys.
'Oh, frabjous day, Quelle heure! Calais!'
They chortled in their joy.

Twas Thursday and the bottom set
Did gyre and gimble in the gym.
All mimsy was Miss Borogrove
And the Head of Maths was *grim*.

Trevor Millum

The Owl and the Pussy-cat

The Owl and the Pussy-cat went to sea
   In a beautiful pea-green boat,
They took some honey, and plenty of money,
   Wrapped up in a five-pound note.
The Owl looked up to the stars above,
   And sang to a small guitar,
'O lovely Pussy! O Pussy, my love,
   What a beautiful Pussy you are,
     You are,
     You are!
   What a beautiful Pussy you are!'

Pussy said to Owl, 'You elegant fowl!
   How charmingly sweet you sing!
O let us be married! too long we have tarried:
   But what shall we do for a ring?'
They sailed away, for a year and a day,
   To the land where the Bong-tree grows
And there in a wood a Piggy-wig stood
   With a ring at the end of his nose,
     His nose,
     His nose,
   With a ring at the end of his nose.

'Dear Pig, are you willing to sell for one shilling
   Your ring?' Said the Piggy, 'I will.'
So they took it away, and were married next day
   By the Turkey who lives on the hill.
They dined on mince, and slices of quince,
   Which they ate with a runcible spoon;
And hand in hand, on the edge of the sand,
   They danced by the light of the moon,
     The moon,
     The moon,
     They danced by the light of the moon.

Edward Lear

The Cook and the Caretaker

(The Cook being rather Owlish,
and the caretaker a real Pussycat.)

The Cook and the Caretaker stirred their tea
And grumbled about the school.
'The children are rude, they play with their food.'
'And the Head is a first-class fool.'
The Cook washed up the Caretaker's cup
And she sighed as she rinsed his spoon,
'How fondly I ache to bake you a cake –
Do you fancy a fresh macaroon,
Aroon,
Aroon,
Do you fancy a fresh macaroon?'

Clare Bevan

Song Thrush Poster

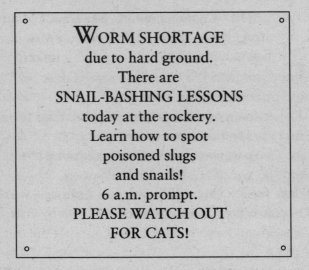

WORM SHORTAGE
due to hard ground.
There are
SNAIL-BASHING LESSONS
today at the rockery.
Learn how to spot
poisoned slugs
and snails!
6 a.m. prompt.
PLEASE WATCH OUT
FOR CATS!

Sue Cowling

Tom Thumb's Diary

Monday: Fell in Mother's pudding bowl! Kicked and struggled so she thought pudding was bewitched and gave it to passing tinker.

Tuesday: Called out 'Bless you!' when tinker sneezed – got thrown into bushes (still in pudding!) for my pains. Ran home – Mother glad to see me. Had bath in teacup to get rid of pudding mixture.

Wednesday: To fields to milk cows with Mother – was tied to a flower stalk for safety. Eaten by cow. Fought and scratched till cow spat me out.

Thursday: Fields again – ploughing with Father. Got lost in furrow. Picked up by eagle (scary!). Flown to seaside and dumped in sea. Swallowed by large fish, caught and presented to King. Everyone surprised to find *me* inside fish!

Friday: Was made official Little Knight of the Court. Fame at last!

Saturday: A bit homesick – asked permission to visit
            Mother and Father for the day. Not sure how
            I'll manage to carry purse full of gold, though.

Sunday: Mother and Father *very* pleased to see me. So
            tired from carrying gold had to stop on way
            back for nap in flowerpot. Luckily butterfly
            passing when woke up so hitched a ride.
            Nobles rushed about trying to catch crazy
            butterfly but no luck. Fell off eventually –
            landed in compost heap. King tickled pink at
            safe return – feasting all next week!

Sue Cowling

There Was a Young Lady of Riga

There was a young lady of Riga
Who went for a ride on a tiger;
They returned from the ride
With the lady inside
And a smile on the face of the tiger.

Anon.

Low Owl

(a univocalic*)

Cold morn: on fork of two o'clock
owl's hoot flows from hood of wood.

Owl's song rolls from blood to brood,
owl's hoot loops on to top of town roofs,
owl's song swoops on strong doors.

Owl's slow whoop – long, forlorn –
soft flood of moon song.

John Rice

*a poem which uses only one of the five vowels: in this case the letter 'o'.

Haiku of the Four Winds

The wind of the north
hurls itself over lonely oceans,
breathing ice into earth's lungs.

The wind from the east
is a sharp-toothed beast, wilfully
biting into day.

The wind from the south
slithers through summer grasses,
made lazy by the sun.

The wind from the west
is a wind of rest, drifting,
whispering from the sunset . . .

Judith Nicholls

The Emperor and the Nightingale

Silent nightingale,
the cage that you occupy
is not the whole world.

Never-a-song songbird,
treated like a clockwork toy,
sing inside your head.

No consolation:
the Emperor too is trapped
with no song to sing.

Mike Jubb

Tanka: Red leaves

Tonight I saw the
caretaker sweeping dead red
   leaves. Whose school is this
Sir? I asked him. He stood up.
Mine . . . and the leaves', he replied.

Fred Sedgwick

December Cinquain

Rainbow
against lead in
the winter sky: a gull
floats on the wind. Starlings rest on
chimneys.

Fred Sedgwick

Kennings

Wild howler
Night prowler
Free mealer
Chicken stealer
Earth liver
Fright giver
Rusty splasher
Hunted dasher
Fox.

Daphne Kitching

Two Witches Discuss Good Grooming

'How do you keep your teeth so green
Whilst mine remain quite white?
Although I rub them vigorously
With cold slime every night.

Your eyes are such a lovely shade
Of bloodshot, streaked with puce.
I prod mine daily with a stick
But it isn't any use.

I envy so, the spots and boils
That brighten your complexion
Even rat spit on my face
Left no trace of infection.

I've even failed to have bad breath
After eating sewage raw,
Yet your halitosis
Can strip paint from a door.'

'My dear, there is no secret,
Now I don't mean to brag.
What you see is nature's work
I'm just a natural hag.'

John Coldwell

In Marble Walls

In marble walls as white as milk,
Lined with a skin as soft as silk;
Within a fountain crystal clear,
A golden apple doth appear.
No doors there are to this stronghold
Yet thieves break in and steal the gold.

Traditional

[Answer: an egg]

One Line Riddles

Golden coin in blue.

*

Many teeth but no bite.

*

Ballet dancer accomplishes the splits.

*

Visionary twins.

*

Muddying the sky.

*

One that holds a thousand.

Pie Corbett

[Answers: Sun, Comb, Scissors, Spectacles, Clouds, Seed.]

My First Is in Two

My first is in two but not in a pair,
My second's in round and also in square;
My third is in heat but never in cold,
My fourth is in new but not in old.
My fifth's not in silver but is in gold,
My sixth is in honest, if the truth be told.
My whole is one strand of the heavenly arc
Where sun and rain meet to leave their mark.

Sue Playdell

[Answer: orange]

A Pin Has a Head

A pin has a head, but has no hair;
A clock has a face, but no mouth there;
Needles have eyes, but they cannot see;
A fly has a trunk without lock or key;
A timepiece may lose, but cannot win;
A corn-field dimples without a chin;
A hill has no leg, but has a foot;
A wine-glass a stem, but not a root;
Rivers run, though they have no feet;
A saw has teeth, but it does not eat;
Ash-trees have keys, yet never a lock;
And a baby crows, without being a cock.

Christina Rossetti

What Am I?

I am a soft boomerang,
That will never spin round.
An unwrapped present,
Found far from the ground.
Don't monkey about –
I live in fear of that.

At a glance, I look
Like a giant's yellow fingers,
But the smell that lingers
Is oh, so much sweeter.

Leave me too long
And I'll turn rotten.
Forgotten – and I'll ooze.

Watch out for my skin –
Or you'll lose your step,
And slip flat
On your back
to crack
Your head wide open.

Pie Corbett

The Tree Spell

January, sleep tight.
February, wake up.

April, come into leaf.
May, open catkins.

June, salute the sun.

September, ripen acorns.
October, let leaves fall.

December, cast spell again.

John Rice

The Months

January cold desolate;
February all dripping wet;
March wind ranges;
April changes;
Birds sing in tune
   To flowers of May,
And sunny June
   Brings longest day;
In scorched July
The storm-clouds fly
Lightning-torn
August bears corn.
September fruit;
In rough October
Earth must disrobe her;
Stars fall and shoot
In keen November;
And night is long
And cold is strong
In bleak December.

Christina Rossetti

Apple Pie

A was an Apple pie
B bit it, C cut it, D dealt it,
E enjoyed it, F fought for it,
G got it, H hoped for it,
I inquired about it,
J jumped on it, K kept it,
L longed for it, M mourned for it,
N nodded at it, O opened it,
P peered in it, Q quartered it,
R ran for it, S sat on it, T took it,
U upset it, V viewed it, W wanted it,
X crossed it, Y yearned for it,
And Z put it in his pocket, and said,
'Well done!'

Anon.

Simple Seasons

Swallows
Primroses
Return.
It's
New,
Green!

Skylarks
Up,
Meadows
Motley,
Elms
Regal.

Apples
Untold,
Trees
Unruly;
Mists
Now.

Waters
Icebound,
Naked
Trees;
Earth
Rests.

Eric Finney

The Witch, the Prince and the Girl in the Tower

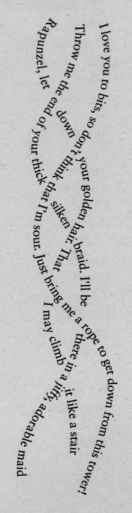

I love you to bits, so don't your golden hair, braid. I'll be
Throw me the down think that silken. That
Rapunzel, let of your thick that I'm sour. Just bring me a rope to get down from this tower!
end there in it like a stair
me a rope to get down from this tower!
sour. Just bring me a there in a jiffy, adorable maid
I may climb a jiffy, adorable maid

Sue Cowling

Litter Lout

Snow

    throws

confetti

       at

everyone

                  Empties

                    out

           litter

           bins

                high

             in

         the

      Snow   air

       shreds

        its

  bus

  tickets

        scatters

          them

   Laughs

      as

        they

     flutter down

  Snow

doesn't

    care

Sue Cowling

My Dad's Amazing!

My dad's *amazing* for he can:

make mountains out of molehills,
teach Granny to suck eggs,
make Mum's blood boil
and then drive her up the wall.

My dad's *amazing* for he also:

walks around with his head in the clouds,
has my sister eating out of his hand,
says he's got eyes in the back of his head
and can read me like a book.

But,
the most *amazing* thing of all is:

when he's caught someone red-handed,
first he jumps down their throat
and then he bites their head off!

Ian Souter

Things to Do on the First Day of the Summer Holidays

Lie in bed late   lounging and lolling about
Eat eggs and bacon   for breakfast at eleven

Sprawl on the lawn   with a long glass of lemonade
Eat salad and seafood   Travel the town T-shirted

Greeting mates   grinning with freedom   Bowl
Bash those bails down   Belt a leather ball

Bouncing to the boundary   bounce bounce   Bring
A take-away home   parathas and poppadums

Talk about treats   sunlight through trees and sand
Sleep in deep silence between sheets   Dream

Fred Sedgwick

Moses

Moses supposes his toeses are roses,
But Moses supposes erroneously;
For nobody's toeses are posies of roses
As Moses supposes his toeses to be.

Anon.

Childhood Tracks

Eating crisp fried fish with plain bread.
Eating sheared ice made into 'snowball'
with syrup in a glass.
Eating young jelly-coconut, mixed
with village-made wet sugar.
Drinking cool water from a calabash gourd
on worked land in the hills.

Smelling a patch of fermenting pineapples
in stillness of hot sunlight.
Smelling mixed whiffs of fish, mango, coffee,
mint, hanging in a market.
smelling sweaty padding lifted off a donkey's back.

Hearing a nightingale in song
in moonlight and sea-sound.
Hearing dawn-crowing of cocks, in answer
to others around the village.
Hearing the laughter
of barefeet children carrying water.
Hearing a distant braying of a donkey
in a silent hot afternoon.
Hearing palmtrees' leaves rattle
on and on at Christmas time.

Seeing a woman walking in loose floral frock.
Seeing a village workman with bag and machete
under a tree, resting, sweat-washed.
Seeing a tangled land-piece of banana trees
with goats in shades cud-chewing.
Seeing a coil of plaited tobacco
like rope, sold, going in bits.
Seeing children playing in schoolyard
between palm and almond trees.
Seeing children toy-making in a yard
while slants of evening sunlight slowly disappear.
Seeing an evening's dusk hour lit up
by dotted lamplight.
Seeing fishing nets repaired between canoes.

James Berry

Mr Khan's Shop

is dark and beautiful.
There are parathas,

garam masala,
nan breads full of fruit.

There are bhajees, samosas, dhal,
garlic, ground cumin seeds.

Shiny emerald chillies
lie like incendiary bombs.

There are bhindi in sacks,
aloo to eat with hot puris

and mango pickle. There's
rice, yogurt,

cucumber and mint –
raita to cool the tongue.

Sometimes you see
where the shop darkens

Mr Khan, his wife
and their children

round the table.
The smells have come alive.

He serves me
poppadums, smiles,

re-enters the dark.
Perhaps one day

he'll ask me to dine with them:
bhajees, samosas, pakoras,

coriander, dhall.
I'll give him this poem: *Sit down*

young man, he'll say
and eat your words.

Fred Sedgwick

What Do You Collect?

What do you collect?
Coins, dolls from other lands?
Or jokes that no one understands?

What do you collect?
Skulls, posters, badges, bells?
Or walking sticks, or seaside shells?

What do you collect?
Stamps, gemstones, model cars?
Or wrappers torn from chocolate bars?

What do you collect?
Leaves, photographs of cats?
Or horror masks and rubber bats?

What do you collect?
Books, fossils, records, rocks?
Or comics in a cardboard box?

Wes Magee

Bonfire Night

Smells of bonfires,
backyards burning –
all the leaves
have finished turning.

Katherine Gallagher

Notes towards a Poem

Sky, grey. Late frost
laces glass, distracts.
Trees, still. Paper, white.

Inside my head
red lava rumbles
in an unquiet earth;
black storm clouds gather,
tigers poise to spring,
a yellowed river
presses at its banks.
Ice binds nothing here
and over lightning flash
and ocean roar
the mountain bursts.
Tigers crash,
white ocean horses
gallop in flood-tide
and down the mountainside
the red-hot torrent pours.

Sky, grey. Late frost.
Trees, laced glass, lost.
Paper, black on white.

Judith Nicholls

A Minute to Midnight

A minute to midnight
and all is still.

For example, these are things that are still:
ornaments, coins, lamp-posts,
the cooker, Major Clark's home for old folk
(just opposite our house, which is also still),
the newsagent's, a hut, soap, tractors,
freshly ironed trousers draped over the chair.

A minute to midnight
and all is still
except for the things that are moving.

Like, for example,
rivers, clouds, leaves, flags,
creaky windmills, lungs, birds' feathers,
digital clocks, grass, the wind,
non-sleeping animals (especially wolves),
planet Earth, the moon, satellites in space,
toenails (well they grow, don't they),
videos that are set to record
programmes in the middle of the night,
washing lines,
mobiles above babies' cots –
and babies' eyelids, they always flicker.

John Rice

Best Places

Hill-tops: when getting there's been tough
And you've earned the view
With leg ache and puff;
Dungeons in castles:
Earth floors, mossy stones –
Stand still and listen
To the chink of chains, the groans!
Waterfalls;
Cool riversides with trees;
Docksides and quays
With the bustle of shipping;
Circuses:
Clowns casually backflipping;
Small, secret beaches
Tucked under a cliff face;
Cathedrals,
Mighty with silence and space;
My grandad's old shed:
I could poke about for hours;
Bridges, belfries, battlements, towers;
Fairgrounds and funfairs –
All thump and throb and glare;

Orchards, hedgerows, cornfields:
The quietness there;
Cities:
I love Edinburgh,
Mum's for Paris and Dad, Rome,
But when all said and done,
        The Best Place is Home.

Eric Finney

The Dream Keeper

Bring me all of your dreams,
You dreamers,
Bring me all of your
Heart melodies
That I may wrap them
In a blue cloud-cloth
Away from the too-rough fingers
Of the world.

Langston Hughes

Dreams

Hold fast to dreams
For if dreams die
Life is a broken-winged bird
That cannot fly

Hold fast to dreams
For when dreams go
Life is a barren field
Frozen with snow.

Langston Hughes

All the world's a stage

All the world's a stage,
And all the men and women merely players:
They have their exits and their entrances;
And one man in his time plays many parts,
His acts being seven ages. At first the infant,
Mewling and puking in the nurse's arms.
And then the whining schoolboy, with his satchel,
And shining morning face, creeping like snail
Unwillingly to school. And then the lover,
Sighing like furnace, with a woeful ballad
Made to his mistress' eyebrow. Then a soldier,
Full of strange oaths, and bearded like the pard,
Jealous in honour, sudden and quick in quarrel,
Seeking the bubble reputation
Even in the cannon's mouth. And then the justice,
In fair round belly with good capon lin'd,
With eyes severe, and beard of formal cut,
Full of wise saws and modern instances;

And so he plays his part. The sixth age shifts
Into the lean and slipper'd pantaloon,
With spectacles on nose and pouch on side,
His youthful hose well sav'd, a world too wide
For his shrunk shank; and his big manly voice,
Turning again toward childish treble, pipes
And whistles in his sound. Last scene of all,
That ends this strange eventful history,
Is second childishness and mere oblivion,
Sans teeth, sans eyes, sans taste, sans everything.

William Shakespeare

Camilla Caterpillar

Camilla Caterpillar kept a caterpillar killer-cat.
A caterpillar killer categorically she kept.
But alas the caterpillar killer-cat attacked Camilla
As Camilla caterpillar catastrophically slept.

Mike Jubb

She Sells Seashells

She sells seashells on the sea shore;
The shells that she sells are seashells I'm sure.
So if she sells seashells on the sea shore,
I'm sure that the shells are sea-shore shells.

Anon.

Barry and Beryl the Bubble Gum Blowers

Barry and Beryl the bubble gum blowers
blew bubble gum bubbles as big as balloons.
All shapes and sizes, zebras and zeppelins,
swordfish and sea lions, sharks and baboons,
babies and buckets, bottles and biplanes,
buffaloes, bees, trombones and bassoons
Barry and Beryl the bubble gum blowers
blew bubble gum bubbles as big as balloons.

Barry and Beryl the bubble gum blowers
blew bubble gum bubbles all over the place.
Big ones in bed, on backseats of buses,
blowing their bubbles in baths with bad taste,
they blew and they bubbled from breakfast till bedtime
the biggest gum bubble that history traced.
One last big breath . . . and the bubble exploded
bursting and blasting their heads into space.
Yes Barry and Beryl the bubble gum blowers
blew bubbles that blasted their heads into space.

Paul Cookson

Having My Ears Boxed

I am waiting in the corridor
To have my ears boxed.
I am nervous, for Mr O'Hanlon
Is a beast of his word.

For the last twenty minutes
I have let my imagination
Run away with itself.
But I am too scared to follow.

Will he use that Swiss Army knife
To slice through cleanly? Bite them off?
Tear carefully along perforated lines?
Tug sharply like loose Elastoplasts?

Acknowledging the crowd's roar
Will he hold my head aloft
As if it were the FA cup
And pull the handles? Aagghhrr . . .

And then the box. Cardboard?
Old cigar-box possibly? Or a pair?
Separate coffins of polished pine.
L and R. 'Gone to a better place.'

Impatient now, I want to get it
Over with. Roll on four o'clock.
When, hands over where-my-ears-used-to-be
I run the gauntlet of jeering kids.

At six, Mother arrives home weary
After a hard day at the breadcrumb factory.
I give her the box. She opens it
And screams something. I say:

'Pardon?'

Roger McGough

Index of First Lines

Index of Poets

Index of Poets

Acknowledgements

The compilers and publishers wish to thank the following for permission to use copyright material:

John Agard, 'The Soldiers Came' from *Laughter is an Egg* by John Agard, Viking (1990), by permission of Caroline Shelden Literary Agency on behalf of the author; Moira Andrew, 'All in the Mind', first published in *Dove on the Roof*, ed. Jennifer Curry, Mammoth (1992), by permission of the author; Les Baynton, 'Stranger', by permission of the author; Hilaire Belloc, 'Progress' from *Complete Verse* by Hilaire Belloc, Random House, by permission of PFD on behalf of the Estate of the author; James Berry, 'Everyday Music' from *A Nest Full of Stars*, Macmillan Children's Books, and 'Childhood Tracks', by permission of PFD on behalf of the author; Clare Bevan, 'The Tudors', first published in *Hysterical Historicals – The Tudors*, ed. Brian Moses, Macmillan Children's Books (2000), 'Coral Reef', first published in *A Sea Creature Ate My Teacher*, ed. Brian Moses, Macmillan Children's Books (2000), and 'The Music Lesson Rap', first published in *The Rhyme Riot*, ed. Gaby Morgan, Macmillan Children's Books (2002), 'The Housemaid's Letter', 'Listen', 'The Cook and the Caretaker' and 'Technology Lesson', by permission of the author; Laurence Binyon, 'For the Fallen (September 1914)', by permission of The Society of Authors on behalf of the author's Estate; Tracey Blance, 'Shame'. Copyright © Tracey Blance 1999, by permission of the author; Valerie Bloom, 'Time' and 'Mega Star Rap', by permission of the author; Ann Bonner, 'Dipa', first published in *Let's Celebrate*, ed. John Foster, Oxford University Press (1989), 'Forest', first published in *Earthwise, Earthways*, ed. Judith Nicholls, Oxford University Press (1993), and 'Music', by permission of the author; Paul Bright, 'Up in Smoke', first published in *Shorts*, ed. Paul Cookson, Macmillan Children's Books (2000), 'The Oojhamaflip', 'Stream Story' and 'King Canute', by permission of the author; Dave Calder, 'Citizen of the World', 'Information for Travellers' and 'The Great Lizards', by permission of the author; James Carter, 'Electric Guitars' from *Cars, Stars and Electric Guitars* by James Carter. Copyright © 2002 James Carter, by permission of Walker Books Ltd; Charles Causley, 'My Mother Saw a Dancing Bear', 'Innocent's Song' and 'Leonardo' from *Collected Poems* by Charles Causley, Macmillan, by permission of David Higham Associates on behalf of the author; Jane Clarke, 'Web of Life', by permission of the author; John Coldwell, 'Two Witches Discuss Good Grooming', first published in *Read Me* 2, ed. Gaby Morgan, Macmillan Children's Books (1999), and 'Cowboy Games and the Good Death', by permission of the author; Andrew Collett, 'Making Music', by permission of the author; Frank Collymore,

Acknowledgements

'Phinniphin', by permission of Ellice Collymore; **Paul Cookson,** 'Barry and Beryl and the Bubble Gum Blowers' from *Tongue Twisters and Tonsil Twizzlers* by Paul Cookson, Solway Publishing (1998), and 'Mathematically Telepathically Magical', first published in *Sing That Joke*, ed. Paul Cookson, Macmillan Children's Books (1998), by permission of the author; **Wendy Cope,** 'The Uncertainty of the Poet' from *Serious Concerns* by Wendy Cope, Faber, by permission of PFD on behalf of the author; **Pie Corbett,** 'Who's That on the Phone?', first published in *Junior Education*, Scholastic. Copyright © Pie Corbett 2000, 'The Day's Eye', first published in *Writer's World*, Heinemann (2001), 'The Wobbling Rainbow', first published in *Junior Education*, Scholastic (2001), 'The Artist's Model Daydreams', 'The Last Wolf Speaks from the Zoo', 'One Line Riddles' and 'What am I?', by permission of the author; **John Cotton,** 'The World with its Countries', by permission of the author; **Sue Cowling,** 'Alien Lullaby' from *Space Poems*, Oxford University Press (2002), 'Houses' from *What Is A Kumquat*, Faber and Faber (1991), 'Song Thrush Poster', 'The Witch, the Prince and the Girl in the Tower', 'Litter Lout', 'Today in Strong Colours' and 'Tom Thumb's Diary', by permission of the author; **Kali Dakos,** 'Why Must it Be Minus 3?' from *Don't Read This Book, Whatever You Do!* by Kali Dakos, by permission of the Simon & Schuster Books for Young Readers, an imprint of Simon & Schuster Children's Publishing Division; **Jan Dean,** 'Dedicating a Baby', 'Prayer for When I'm Cross' and 'The Unit of Sleep', by permission of the author; **Peter Dixon,** 'Problem Solving', 'My Daddy Dances Tapstep', 'Modern Art' and 'Grown-Ups', by permission of the author; **Lord Alfred Douglas,** 'The Shark', by permission of John Rubinstein and John Stratford, Joint Literary Executors of the Estate of the author; **Gina Douthwaite,** 'Divorce' and 'A Crack Band', by permission of the author; **Helen Dunmore,** 'What Shall I Draw?' from *Secrets* by Helen Dunmore, by permission of A P Watt Ltd on behalf of the author; **Gwen Dunn,** 'Dandelions', by permission of the author; **Sun Dymoke,** 'Scissors', by permission of the author; **Ivy O. Eastwick,** 'Thanksgiving' from *Cherry Stones! Garden Swings* by Ivy Eastwick, by permission of Abingdon Press; **Richard Edwards,** 'If I Were the Conductor' from *I Wish I Were a Teabag* by Richard Edwards, Viking (1990), by permission of the author; **Eleanor Farjeon,** 'Poetry' from *Blackbird Has Spoken* by Eleanor Farjeon, Macmillan, and 'J is for Jazz-Man' from *Silver Sand and Snow*, Michael Joseph, by permission of David Higham Associates on behalf of the Estate of the author; **Laurence Ferlinghetti,** 'The World is a Beautiful Place' from *A Coney Island of the Mind* by Laurence Ferlinghetti. Copyright © 1955 by Laurence Ferlinghetti, by permission of New Directions Publishing Corporation; **Rachel Field,** 'The Hills' from *Branches Green* by Rachel Field. Copyright © 1934 Macmillan Publishing Company, renewed copyright © 1962 Arthur Pederson, by permission of the Simon & Schuster Books for Young Readers, an imprint of Simon Schuster Children's Publishing Division; **Eric Finney,** 'Simple Seasons', 'Best Places', 'Thank You Letter' and 'Finding Magic', by permission of the author, **Aileen Fisher,** 'Light the Fesitve Candles' from *Skip Around the Year* by Aileen Fisher. Copyright © 1967, 1995 Aileen Fisher, by permission of Marian Reiner on behalf of the author; **John Foster,** 'Mowers', first published in *Four O'Clock Friday,* Oxford University Press. Copyright © 1991 John Foster, 'Summer Storm' from *Standing on the Sidelines,* Oxford University Press. Copyright © 1995 John Foster, 'It Hurts' from *Making Waves,* Oxford University Press. Copyright © 1997 John Foster, by permission of the author; **Katherine Gallagher,** 'Bonfire Night', by permission of the author; **Zulfikar Ghose,** 'Geography Lesson', by permission of Sheil Land Associates Ltd on behalf of the author; **Chrissie Gittens,** 'The Powder Monkey', 'The British Museum Print Room' from *Pilot,* Dagger Press (2001), by permission of the author; **Mary Green,** 'Teacher's Torture', 'Pyramid Pie', 'Excuses', 'Volcano', 'Seaside Sonata' and 'Mouse Laughing', by permission of the author; **Philip Gross,** 'This is a Recorded Message' from *Scratch City* by Philip Gross, by permission of Faber and Faber Ltd; **David Harmer,** 'Our Tree', 'On The Streets', 'The News', 'Dobbo's First Swimming Lesson' and 'Cutpurse Kit', by permission of the author; **Trevor Harvey,** 'Printout, Wipe Out', first published in *Techno Talk,* compiled by Trevor Harvey , Bodley Head (1994), 'Growing Up in the 1930's', first published in 'How We Used to Live', *Projects Magazine,* Scholastic (2001), 'The Hedgehog' and 'Breath', by permission of the author, **Seamus Heaney,** 'Mid-Term Break' from *Death of a Naturalist* by Seamus Heaney, by permission of Faber and Faber Ltd; **Adrian Henri,** 'Notes for an Autumn Painting' from *Adrian Henri – Collected Poems,* Allison and Busby (1986). Copyright © Adrian Henri 1986, by permission of Rogers, Coleridge & White on behalf of the author; **Lee Bennett Hopkins,** 'Staring' from *Been to Yesterdays* by Lee Bennett Hopkins. Copyright © 1995 Lee Bennett Hopkins, by permission from Boyds Mills Press; **Libby Houston,** 'Post-War' from *Cover of Darkness, Selected Poems 1961-1998* by Libby Houston, Slow Dancer Press. Copyright © Libby Houston (1967) 1999, by permission of the author; **Langston Hughes,** 'Mother to Son', 'Carol of the Brown King', 'Aunt Sue's Stories', 'Dreams, 'The Dream Keeper' and 'Song for a Banjo Dance' from *Selected Poems* by Langston Hughes, by permission of David Higham Associates on behalf of the author; **Ted Hughes,** 'Robin Song' from *Crow* by Ted Hughes, by permission of Faber and Faber Ltd; **Robert Hull,** 'Maths Person' from *Stargazer* by Robert Hull, Hodder, by permission of PFD on behalf of the author; **Elizabeth Jennings,** 'Friends' and 'A Sort of Chinese Poem' from *Collected Poems* by Elizabeth Jennings, Carcanet, by permission of David Higham Associates on behalf of the author; **Mike Johnson,** 'Tall Story', first published in *The Upside-Down Frown,* ed. Andrew Peters Fusek, Wayland (1999), 'Science Lesson', first published in *Ridiculous Rhymes,* ed. John Foster, Collins (2001), 'Missing' and 'Natural Numbers', by permission of the author; **Mina Johnson,** 'Points of View', by permission of the author; **Mike Jubb,** 'We got Rhyme', first published in *A Poetry Teacher's Toolkit, Vol. 2, Rhymes, Rhythms and Rattles* by Collette Drifte and Mike Jubb Fulton (2002), 'The Emperor and the Nightingale', first published in *A Poetry*

Acknowledgements

Teachers' Toolkit, Vol. 3, Style, Shape and Structure by Collette Drifte and Mike Jubb Fulton (2002), and 'Camilla Caterpillar', by permission of the author; **Jackie Kay**, 'Divorce', by permission of the author; Penny Kent, 'Arturi's Story', 'Winter Seeds' and 'A Sense of History', by permission of the author; **Penny Kent**, 'Arturi's Story', 'Winter Seeds' and 'A Sense of History', by permission of the author; **Jean Kenward**, 'Mela', by permission of the author; **James Kirkup**, 'The Sand Artist' and 'First Art Lesson', by permission of the author; **Daphne Kitching**, 'Job Description' and 'Kennings' from *As long as there are trees* by Daphne Kitching, Kingston Press (2001), by permission of the author; **John Kitching**, 'My Teacher Taught Me How to See', first published in *Schools Out*, compiled by John Foster, Oxford University Press (1988), 'Short Livers', first published in *Hysterical Historical Poems*, compiled by Brian Moses (2000), 'History', 'Science Graveyard', 'A Bit of a Problem', 'Historian', 'Art Year Haikus', 'Geography' and 'Matchstick King', by permission of the author; **Karla Kuskin**, 'Lewis Has a Trumpet' from *In the Middle of the Trees* by Karla Kuskin. Copyright © 1959, renewed 1986 by Karla Kuskin; and 'Counting' from *The Rose on My Cake* by Karla Kuskin, copyright © 1964, renewed 1992 by Karla Kuskin, by permission of Scott Treimel NY on behalf of the author; **Una Leavy**, 'Go-cart', by permission of the author; **Pat Leighton**, 'Bullied', 'Wonder Birds', 'Voice from the Pharaoh's Tomb', 'My First Dog', 'Snail' and 'Printer's Devil', by permission of the author; **Myra Cohn Livingston**, 'Shell' from *Worlds I Know and Other Poems* by Myra Cohn Livingston, McElderry Books/Artheneum. Copyright © 1986 Myra Cohn Livingston, by permission of Marian Reiner on behalf of the author; **Roger McGough**, 'Having my Ears Boxed' and 'The Boyhood of Raleigh', by permission of PFD on behalf of the author; **Lindsay MacRae**, 'The Funeral' from *How to Avoid Kissing Your Parents in Public* by Lindsay MacRae, Puffin (2000). Copyright © Lindsay MacRae, 2000, by permission of the author; **Wes Magee**, 'What do you collect?' 'What is a million?' and 'The Electronic House', by permission of the author; **John Masefield**, 'Cargoes', by permission of The Society of Authors as the Literary Representative of the Estate of the author; **Trevor Milum**, 'Jabbermockery', by permission of the author; **Adrian Mitchell**, 'Techno Child' from *Balloon Lagoon and the Magic Islands of Poetry* by Adrian Mitchell, by permission of PFD on behalf of the author; **Tony Mitton**, 'Hunting the Leaven Passover', included in *Festivals*, ed. Andrew Fusek Peters, by permission of David Higham Associates on behalf of the author; **Pat Moon**, 'Earth's Clock' from *Earthlines* by Pat Moon, Pimlico (1993), by permission of the author; **Michaela Morgan**, 'Blake's Tyger – revisisted', by permission of the author; **Brian Moses**, 'The Group', first published in *Turn that Racket Down*, ed. Paul Cookson, Red Fox (2001). Copyright © Brian Moses, 'Entering a Castle' from *Don't Look at Me in that Tone of Voice*, poems by Brian Moses, Macmillan (1998). Copyright © Brian Moses, 'Behind the Staffroom Door' from *The Secret Life of Teachers*, ed. Brian Moses, Macmillan (1996). Copyright © Brian Moses, 'Names' from *Knock Down Ginger and Other Poems* by Brian Moses,

Acknowledgements

Cambridge University Press (1994). Copyright © Brian Moses, 'If I Were a Shape' and 'It's Not the Same Without Dad', by permission of the author; **Jeff Moss,** 'The Last Day of School' from *The Other Side of the Door* by Jeff Moss, Bantam Books, by permission of ICM, Inc on behalf of the author; **Frances Nagle,** 'My Gang' and 'Dream Team', first published in *My Gang*, ed. Brian Moses, Macmillan (1999), 'Silver Moon' and 'Star Turn', by permission of the author; **Judith Nicholls,** 'Remembrance Day', 'Haiku of the Four Winds', 'Notes towards a Poem', 'Dolphin Dance', 'First Television', 'Drum' and 'Plague Frogs'. Copyright © Judith Nicholls 2002, by permission of the author; **Grace Nichols,** 'Give Yourself a Hug' from *Give Yourself a Hug.* Copyright © 1994 by Grace Nichols, by permission of Curtis Brown Ltd, London, on behalf of the author; **Gareth Owen,** 'The New House', 'Friends', 'Space Shot' and 'Jonah and the Whale' from *Collected Poems for Children* by Gareth Owen, Macmillan Children's Books (2000). Copyright © Gareth Owen 2000, by permission of Rogers, Coleridge & White on behalf of the author; **Brian Patten,** 'Burying the Dog in the Garden' and 'Embryonic Mega-Stars' from *Gargling with Jelly* by Brian Patten, Viking (1985). Copyright © Brian Patten, 1985, by permission The Penguin Group (UK) Ltd; and 'Bringing up a Single Parent', 'Three Frazzles in a Frimple' and 'Geography Lesson' from *Juggling With Gerbils* by Brian Patten, Puffin Books (2000). Copyright © Brian Patten 2000, by permission of Rogers, Coleridge & White on behalf of the author; **Mervyn Peake,** 'Disembarkation Chorus' from *Peake's Progress*, ed. M. Gilmore, Penguin, by permission of David Higham Associates on behalf of the author; **Joan Poulson,** 'Jacob and the Angel', 'Dragonflies', 'Wilderness' and 'All That Space', by permission of the author; **Janis Priestley,** 'Just One Wish', by permission of the author; **John Rice,** 'A Minute to Midnight', first published in *The Great Escape – A World Book Day Poetry Book*, Macmillan Children's Books (2000), 'Low Owl' and 'Cousins', first published in *Bears Don't Like Bananas*, Hodder Wayland (1991), 'Mr Mizen', 'Constant, Constant Little Light', 'The Tree Spell', 'The Machine of the Three Big Ears' and 'Gannet Diving', by permission of the author; **E V Rieu,** 'The Paint Box', by permission of the Authors Licensing & Collecting Society Ltd on behalf of the estate of the author; **Coral Rumble,** 'Guess Who?', first published in *The Works*, ed. Peter Cookson, Macmillan Children's Books (2000), 'Sometimes' and 'New Frontiers', by permission of the author; **Anita Marie Sackett,** 'Rain', *Seam Poetry Magazine*, 14 (2001), by permission of the author; **Clive Sansom,** 'The Train', by permission of David Higham Associates on behalf of the author; **Fred Sedgwick,** 'First Thing Today', 'Mr Khan's Shop', 'December Cinquain', 'Red Leaves', 'Things to Do on the First Day of the Summer Holidays' and 'After Giacometti', by permission of the author; **Danielle Sensier,** 'New Girl' and 'experiment', by permission of the author; **Ian Serraillier,** 'Mountains', by permission of Anne Serraillier; **Ian Souter,** 'From My Window', 'Heavy Metal, Stormy Weather', 'My Dad's Amazing', 'Early Last Sunday' and 'Numberless', by permission of the author; **Kenneth C. Steven,** 'Mushrooms',

Acknowledgements

by permission of the author; **Roger Stevens**, 'Julius Caesar's Last Breakfast' from *I Did Not Eat the Goldfish* by Roger Stevens, Macmillan Children's Books (2002), 'The Most Important Rap', first published in *Performance Poems*, ed. Brian Moses, Southgate Publishers Ltd (1996), 'The Dawdling Dog', 'Chalk', 'The Museum Says' and 'The Art Gallery Says', by permission of the author; **Véronique Tadjo**, 'Friendship' from *Talking Drums*, ed. Véronique Tadjo, by permission of A & C Black (Publishers) Ltd; **Rabindranath Tagore**, 'Day by Day I Float My Paper Boats' from *Collected Poems and Plays of Rabindranath Tagore*, by permission of Visva-Bharati University, Calcutta; **Charles Thomson**, 'Name-calling' and 'Counting Horrors', by permission of the author; **James Tippett**, 'Building a Skyscraper' from *Crickety Cricket! The Best Loved Poems of James S Tippett* by James Tippett. Copyright © 1933, renewed 1973 by Martha K. Tippett, by permission of HarperCollins Publishers, Inc; **Steve Turner**, 'In the Beginning' from *The Day I Fell Down the Toilet*, Lion Publishing (1996), 'With My Hands' and 'Hickory Digital Clock' from *Dad, You're Not Funny*, Lion Publishing (1999), by permission of the author; **Jennifer Tweedie**, 'Ocean Travel', first published in *Another Very First Poetry Book*, Oxford University Press (1992), by permission of the author; **Judith Viorst**, 'Some Things Don't Make Sense at All' and 'It's a Wonderful Life' from *If I Were in Charge of the World and Other Worries* (1981). Copyright © Judith Viorst 1981, 'Harvey' and 'Someday Someone Will Bet That You Can't Name All Fifty States' from *Sad Underwear* by Judith Vorist, by permission of A M Heath & Co Ltd on behalf of the author; **Philip Waddell**, 'Important Notice', 'Puzzler' and 'In the Garden', by permission of the author; **Barrie Wade**, 'Haiku Calendar: Southern Version', by permission of the author; **Celia Warren**, 'A Liking for the Viking' and 'Roman Invasions', by permission of the author; **David Whitehead**, 'My Pet Mouse', first published in *Pet Poems*, ed. Jennifer Curry, Scholastic (2001), by permission of the author; **Brenda Williams**, 'Jack Frost', by permission of the author; **Kit Wright**, 'All of Us' from *Great Snakes* by Kit Wright, Penguin (1994), by permission of the author; **Benjamin Zephaniah**, 'Fearless Bushmen' from *Wicked World* by Benjamin Zephaniah, Puffin (2000). Copyright © Benjamin Zephaniah, 2000, by permission of The Penguin Group (UK) Ltd.

Every effort has been made to trace the copyright holders but if any have been inadvertently overlooked the publishers will be pleased to make the necessary arrangement at the first opportunity.